BLIND SPOT

Illuminating the
Hidden Value of Business

Steve Diller, Nathan Shedroff, and Sean Sauber

TWO WAVES

BOOKS

TWO WAVES BOOKS

BROOKLYN, NY, USA

Blind Spot
Illuminating the Hidden Value in Business
By Steve Diller, Nathan Shedroff, and Sean Sauber

Two Waves Books
an Imprint of Rosenfeld Media, LLC
457 Third Street, #4R
Brooklyn, New York
11215 USA

On the Web: twowavesbooks.com
Please send errors to: errata@twowavesbooks.com

Publisher: Louis Rosenfeld
Managing Editor: Marta Justak
Editors: Joe Shepter and Susan Hobbs
Illustrations: Nathan Shedroff
Interior Layout Tech: Danielle Foster
Cover and Interior Design: The Heads of State
Indexer: Sharon Shock
Proofreader: Sue Boshers

ISBN: 1-933820-69-1
ISBN-13: 978-1-933820-69-9
LCCN: 2016939711

Printed and bound in the United States of America

This book is dedicated to the memory of
Ernst Toch, who heard the music in innovation
and made this book possible.

Contents at a Glance

Contents and Executive Summary

Presents the concept of premium value and its connection to overall stock valuation and consumer loyalty.

Discusses the types of relationships that companies can have with customers, and why relationships are the key to the companies' underlying value.

How companies can use evocative language to gain clarity on what kind of relationship they need to build with customers and to design it.

Elaborates on the visualization tool called a *waveline*, which makes it possible to get a full understanding of the type of relationship that should be built over time that will lead to far greater market valuation.

Shows how to organize a company's innovation process to maximize successful relationship-building with customers.

Foreword

I normally hate books like this. I don't want to have a customer experience, much less a brand experience. I can't bring myself to support any effort to give corporations a human face to match their ill-begotten rights of citizenship and personhood. Companies are enough like people already, and people are becoming far too much like brands themselves.

But Nathan Shedroff (whom I've discussed these issues with) and his co-authors, Steve Diller and Sean Sauber, are more forgiving people than I am, and they see a way for companies to humanize their operations without resorting to yet more manipulation. In fact, the guiding principle here is not that corporations should ape human behaviors in order to manipulate consumers into behaving more predictably. That's the conventional wisdom in the customer experience universe, and it's what has led to increasing alienation of human beings from the companies that mean to reduce their customers' autonomy and individuality in the name of short-term profit.

Rather, the authors suggest that companies accept their essentially non-human status and embrace the humanity of the people buying from and working for them. The corporation is not the ends but the means.

That may be the greatest blind spot of all in today's business landscape and, ironically, the one that our digital technologies have made most apparent to everyone else. In such an environment, transparency seems to alert everyone else to our own shortcomings, while hiding them from us.

Thinking long and hard about one's customers' experiences—from first point of contact through sale and word-of-mouth to social responsibility, labor relations, and environmental impact—may be the best way for a company to justify actually benefiting people in the long run. Yes, it's good for business.

—Douglas Rushkoff
Author, *Throwing Rocks at the Google Bus*

1

A World of Hidden Value

On July 14, 2014, an Engadget editor named Ryan Block and his wife called to cancel their Comcast cable and Internet service. During an 18-minute phone call (only 8 of which were recorded), a Comcast customer service representative badgered them with questions and refused to do the simple task they asked. The entire conversation consisted of exchanges like the following:

Block: "I'd like to disconnect."

Service rep: "Help me understand why you don't want faster Internet."

Block: "Help me understand why you just can't disconnect us."

Service rep: "Because my job is to have a conversation with you...about keeping your service."

This went on until the bemused Block wondered aloud, "Am I being punked?"

For those of you outside of North America, Comcast is a cable TV and Internet company that frequently tops the lists of the worst companies on the continent. Its most obvious problem is the terrible relationships it has with its customers. Many people simply hate dealing with the company.

Part of the blame falls on the industry: almost all cable and Internet companies in the United States fare poorly in customer surveys. Still, part of the blame has to fall on the company itself. Comcast offers an array of conflicting and confusing promotions. The deals routinely end 12 months after they begin, triggering huge increases in prices that surprise customers. Then, if you try to disconnect, the company makes you cancel over the phone, where you'll find a customer service rep trained to do nearly anything to keep you as a customer. And after you cancel their services, the company often doesn't stop billing your account until you physically return equipment to the nearest store, which may not be nearby.

Worse still, customer service reps often act like Block's did. He may as well have been a robot—he had a script, and he stuck to it. His compensation was likely based on how many customers he could prevent from discontinuing service. In an ordinary interaction, people respond to one another. If a person seems upset, you don't start telling jokes. If they're happy, you're happy for them. You build relationships using empathy, not by stubbornly saying the same thing over and over, regardless of what the other person says.

Over time, emotional experiences add up. If you have one interaction after another that leaves you feeling worse, it will result in a bad relationship. When that happens, you talk about the company in the same way that you talk about a person you can't stand: obtuse, frustrating, and annoying. You can actually come to hate a business. And when you get a chance to get rid of its services, you dump it, just as you might dump a friend or romantic partner. (The same is true in the positive, too: you might love and admire a company based on the kinds of interactions you have with them.)

That said, you might ask why Comcast is still in business. Because it's lucky. It has a virtual monopoly in some regions and competes with only one or two rivals in the rest of the regions. Its competitors all engage in the same unpleasant practices, so consumers have to pick their poison. But most companies have no such luxury. If Comcast were a neighborhood restaurant, it wouldn't last more than a few months. Within days of opening, anyone who went there would tell everyone else to stay away.

In fact, most small businesses understand that their customers have a series of experiences that turn into a *relationship*. They know that developing positive relationships is critical to their success. They have to learn their customers' names, understand their preferences, and know what their customers want before they say so. Their business has to be positive, upbeat, and sensitive. Being good at what they do simply isn't enough. They have to know how to give and take in a two-way conversation. They have to care.

Blind Spots and Opportunities

You'll find that this is just one of many blind spots that businesses have. In Comcast's case, short-term profit is much more important than long-term relationships, and holding customers prisoner is the only acceptable corporate strategy. Comcast prefers to incentivize management and front-line employee alike to make it nearly impossible for customers to leave (although, ultimately, it's no more difficult than a call to their credit card company to cancel the account) than to give its customers a reason to *want* to be customers for the long term.

This is just one way in which traditional business thinking has blinded its practitioners to reality. Relationships are the source of long-term value, not merely because it's easier to keep an existing customer than to acquire a new one, but because satisfied customers help a business acquire new ones.

It's really no different than personal relationships. While the healthy relationships you forge with friends and family are built more on emotional and meaningful value, the same is still true of relationships built on financial and functional value. For some strange reason, businesspeople have been told that only the short-term, financial value is worth building, but any wise businessperson knows this isn't the case. Still, traditional business literature is rife with this contradiction.

Broadly speaking, everyone has at least some blind spots. This reference indicates an area of the retina (the inside back of your eyeballs), which has no light-sensitive rods and cones because it's where all of the other optic nerves flow out of the eye and into the brain. This creates a small disc in your field of view that has no actual information, although your brains are facile in filling in the missing signals with assumed data that makes it seem like you're getting a complete, seamless picture of our surroundings. You don't really notice that you're not really seeing some of the data around you.

Likewise, organizations often have blind spots that they don't notice because their managements "fill in" what's missing with alternative perspectives, or they ignore missing data because they can't make sense of it themselves. Unfortunately, this process is often filled in with dogma and not experience. Unlike what our brains are capable of doing, these blind spots cause companies to miss important cues, obscure lucrative opportunities, and assume they have the complete picture when they're leaving dollars on the table, because they never see what they don't look for.

The blind spot we're most interested in here has to do with what contributes to companies' total value, namely, the building of relationships with customers Without seeing relationships for what they are—a mutual appreciation built on sequences of pleasing customer experiences over time—organizations miss what is often the single most important opportunity to build their total value (see Chapter 2, "Defining a Business Relationship," for more information).

Relationships and Opportunities

What defines a relationship with a company instead of another person? Put simply, it's a connection with a company that someone values. You can use a product to do a task, but for many of the things you own and use, you don't value them beyond their functions. A relationship is different. It grows out of the customer's interactions with your company. It can be quite strong and even have human dimensions, and it's an opportunity for a company to create a long-term customer.

Such a definition may seem strange or overstated, but research has shown that people see and react to brands and businesses much as they do to other people. In the 1990s, for example, Stanford researchers Cliff Nass and Byron Reeves found that users of devices such as computers and microwave ovens often treated these objects as if they were human. In other words, they used a shorthand with these objects that granted them a kind of "virtual personhood."[1] Everyone knows that a microwave isn't a person, nor a computer, but it's much easier to treat it as if it were—and to expect the same treatment, in kind. This grants the device (or company) the permission to have and express emotions, personalities, and even agency—but only as long as it acts like like a decent human being. The moment the company crosses the social boundaries

1. Nass and Reeves' tests showed that even really smart graduate students at one of the best universities in the world performed this shorthand. It's not something that only naïve or inexperienced people do. They showed that complex interactions resulting in trust, persuasion, and allegiance could all be created through very simple tasks with computers. In just one example, they found that a computer that flattered itself in very simple language, after performing a routine web search, garnered distrust and disgust, just as if a person had flattered itself. However, if a second computer flattered the first (the one performing the search), the operator thought more highly of both (the one that had been praised and the one doing the praising). This exactly mimics Western human behavior. Nearly any complex social relationship can be modeled between people and devices, and fascinatingly, they still hold true.

of acceptable behavior (like ignoring your pleas to cancel your service), the same power that builds brand value allows it to be destroyed—even faster. That colleague you trust at work, that you treat with respect? Once you find him to be a purposeful impediment to your own tasks, he's no longer an ally but an adversary—or even an enemy. This is the nature of human relationships, and it's the same with how you expect devices, services, and organizations to behave. The value you grant them (or revoke) is entirely built on the relationships you build.

In a ground-breaking study in 1998, Susan Fournier (a noted management scholar and researcher on brand value) argued that brands and customers do forge meaningful relationships. The reason is fairly simple. We're human, and as humans, it's what we do. We grow up learning how to forge relationships with other people. When we interact with products or companies, we default to what comes naturally.

Of course, products and companies aren't people. It may not make sense to love Disney, or you may be disappointed that the creator of a mobile device espouses a cause you dislike, but it happens. You might get angry and frustrated at a vending machine. You possibly love shoes or one of your home appliances. You may feel like you're greeting an old friend returning from a trip abroad when you crack open your favorite soda. It's how humans make sense of the complex world around them. It's just how we are.

Unfortunately, most companies don't understand this tactic and don't invest in relationships, at least not in a continuous, strategic way. It's easy to understand why. Relationships are fuzzy, not easily measured, and they mean different things to different people. Marketers talk about them, but few businesses treat them as strategic assets. Walk into a boardroom, and you can get a long way talking about income statements, P&L, CapEx, and ROI. Talk about relationships, and few people want to listen, especially if the business isn't doing well. When challenged, there's not yet any way to point to the value of relationships in an organization's financials because the value is spread throughout *all* of the statements. It doesn't feel real, but it's encapsulated everywhere a company does business. Relationships don't seem real or concrete enough to act upon. They're seen as a byproduct of other activities, something that happens on their own as long as you take care of other things.

For most businesses, relationships are a major factor in building what's known as *premium value*. Premium value indicates how much more a customer would pay for one product or service over an equivalent replacement. A relationship-conscious company like Disney can charge much more per visit to its parks than Six Flags. Coke sells for more than generic soda. And Apple can charge much more than its rivals for products that do much the same thing.

You might think we're merely talking about one product being better than another. That's not the entire story, though, as good relationships start with products that work. But functionality is table stakes these days, and premium brands don't stress functional attributes. Almost any company can build products that do what they're supposed to do, or it can offer unique features that don't really matter. However, most companies have to compete on price, and relatively few understand how to create the kinds of experiences that build a durable relationship that customers value and that transcend price.

Five Types of Premium Value

Functional value is usually easy to quantify. Anytime a company stresses a particular feature of its offering (or how many there are), or the performance of the product or service as a whole, it is communicating about functional value. This is the first consideration customers usually make, and it's a great differentiator—unless some other company offers a slightly better feature or just one more. Functional value is usually easy to communicate, but it almost never engenders loyalty because it's the shallowest kind of value that can be provided to someone.

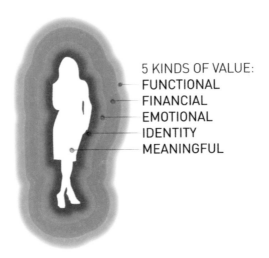

5 KINDS OF VALUE:
FUNCTIONAL
FINANCIAL
EMOTIONAL
IDENTITY
MEANINGFUL

Financial value is the second kind, and it's a little more involved, creating a slightly deeper connection between a customer and a company (though not by much). When the number of choices is narrowed by various options, consumers turn to issues of money: how much are buyers really willing to spend for certain function or performance? Everyone has a different answer, which is why there are so many options for cars, computers, types of hand soap, and everything in between—at all price levels.

Because they're easy to measure quantitatively, both functional and financial values are pretty easy to see and understand. Either a product or service has the function a consumer wants or not. Either it's within a set budget or not. Most see the process of deciding what to buy or use as rational. These types of value, because they're quantifiable and, in a sense, visible—since they operate at a material level—are the least significant for consumers and provide the least sustainable source of differentiation for companies. They're about as basic as value gets, so buyers refer to them as, well...basic.

The other three forms of value are entirely different, however. This makes them complicated and difficult to work with. Ironically, these forms of value are just where the greatest opportunities to differentiate in the market reside. They're also the most important source of stock valuation. Havas Media, for instance, has determined that companies that consistently offer these types of value are, on average, valued significantly higher by the markets. Because of this, and because they offer so much greater benefits to customers, which leads to sustainable competitive advantage, these are thought of as the source of premium value.

The third kind of value is *emotional value*. Everyone acknowledges that emotions exist, yet some in business are still unable to see their impact on customer decisions. A "just-the-facts-ma'am" approach doesn't allow room for emotions to enter the equation. Yet, emotions are not only deeper in the relationships between customers and companies (and between individuals, too), but they're also very much a type of value that gets exchanged, even if they feel invisible. It's also easy to explain: consumers are willing to pay more for those experiences that provide them with the emotions they seek. That's all there is to it, but it flies in the face of traditionalists who insist that "people won't pay more for things than they have to."

Of course, every good salesperson knows that they're selling on the basis of emotions more than on price or performance. It's why consumers end up with a choice that's often over their budget or doesn't meet all of the functional needs they've specified. What drives decisions, in these cases, is that the choice makes the buyer feel greater, younger, happier, thinner, more accomplished, sexier—something. That's incredibly powerful and starts to explain the discrepancy between the book value of a company (the simple tally of its assets and liabilities) and its brand value (which is usually many times higher). This isn't a nefarious thing, by the way. We're usually after satisfaction more than features or price, in the first place.

Contrary to being irrational, emotions often aren't. You may not have realized you had a deep need to feel younger, more active, more successful, but if you respond positively to offerings that make you feel those things, that's a pretty rational response. The difference is that the decision drivers, at this stage, are no longer so easy to spot, can't be easily defined, and can't be easily measured quantitatively. Because they're not measured, often management is blind to them. The result is huge missed opportunities that are never even seen.

The fourth type of value is *identity value,* and this governs decisions in terms of what consumers feel fits who they are. Some people are Nike folks; others Adidas; still others identify with Puma or New Balance or Lululemon. Some come from cultural backgrounds that instruct them to only purchase brands that will advance their cultural communities or causes.

Even those who eschew brands react on this level. It may not be healthy to align a personal identity with brands—or construct self-images and identities from brands—but consumers do. They gravitate to things that complement who they feel they are and align with personal values. Like all premium types of value, this decision driver often acts uncon-sciously and, because humans don't change their sense of self often, it's even more powerful and stable than emotional value. For example, if you're a conservative, a liberal, an agnostic, a Canadian, a Yankee's fan, or a fanboy of anything (in short, anything you put after "I am a..."), this particular type of value lives in this space.

Whereas many business people recognize that identity value exists, they often manage it in a haphazard way because they can't easily quantita-tively measure its importance, as they can with price and performance. Frequently, they hand off its management to the marketing and advertis-ing folks, who are given at least a bit of a pass on justifying what they do on quantitative grounds. The attitude seems to be, "Well, we can't really measure this, but we know it matters, so let's just let the brand people do their thing and hope it pays off." The blind spot here is even more signifi-cant, and the lack of rigor in addressing it can be deeply disconcerting for anyone who has to answer for investment choices.

Finally, there's *meaningful value*, which transcends the other types of premium value in significance to customers. It is the deepest, most stable value that gets exchanged between people. In the past, it was mostly exchanged between individuals or between people and institutions like churches or government. Now, however, corporations and organizations of all types play this role in daily life. At this level, it's not so much about who you are but about how you see the world around you. This is governed by 15 core meanings (see Chapter 7, "Discovering," for an explanation of core meanings).

People's core meanings drive decisions about who they're friends with, what jobs they'll take, what they buy, and what they read, watch, and play. Whether you see the world as a scary, terrible, dangerous, wondrous, friendly, or hilarious place, that belief lives at this level and when you can surround yourself with people and things that reinforce this view, you're more satisfied and, as a consumer, willing to pay a lot more. Prius owners and survivalists, alike, are driven by different core meanings at this level.

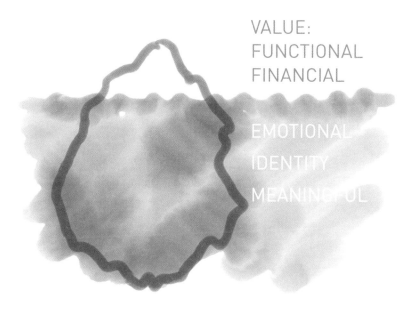

VALUE:
FUNCTIONAL
FINANCIAL

EMOTIONAL
IDENTITY
MEANINGFUL

Premium Value Is Real Value

While it's more difficult to measure and it's not a traditional business approach, premium value is very real and definitely valuable. If they make no place for it, business people are actively blinding themselves to the highest value there is in the market.

Not everyone pays more for premium value in everything they buy. Most have certain categories in which these types of value mean more to them—and some they couldn't care less about—for example, Porsche and Cartier, Hilton and Nike, Apple and Whole Foods.

These, of course, are generalizations. But some people care deeply about the food they eat; others just consider it food. Some give great care to the clothes, accessories, hair and makeup they put on; others eschew these for more generic choices. The point is that your customers engage on premium levels for many, but not all, things, and it's your job to understand which.

All of the above examples are evidence that premium value exists. It's often difficult to tease the five values apart, in the wild, since all five are active at all times (potentially). And all are part of what makes a relationship engaging, attractive, and valuable. No company that wowed investors with huge valuations on an IPO or sale did so on the basis of functional and financial value alone. In fact, for most companies, the more premium value you generate, the bigger the share it has of your overall value. If you're innovating to drive growth and value in a company, the best kind to focus on is premium value. And, you can't get there focusing only on features and price.

There are rare opportunities to "see" this value distinctly when a company goes public or is acquired by, or merges with, another. At these moments, the balance and income statements of a company are distinctly different before and after the sale. For example, when Instagram was purchased by Facebook in April 2012, the "books" said that

Instagram (then only 13 people) was worth around $86 million. This represented their total assets (including a $50 million investment the week prior to purchase).

The company was "valued" at $500 million before the sale, but this wasn't a real number, just a guess, based on past valuations of similar companies. According to the book, if the company had to shut down and sell everything off, it was only worth that $86 million.

But Facebook bought Instagram for $1.1 billion! That's a huge difference! Why did Facebook pay almost 13 times that $86 million figure? Where did that value exist in the company's financial statements? It was even double the amount that Instagram's investors guessed the company was worth.

We contend that the extra $1 billion that Instagram received in the sale *was* the result of the premium value it had built. Before the sale, this extra billion dollars didn't appear to exist and wasn't tracked, nor was it trackable. The day after the sale was final, however, that extra $1 billion was very real and had to be put into the balance sheet somewhere—and there's a special catch-all cell just for these things. It's called "goodwill" and it's a place to shove the extra money companies make when they're purchased or offer their IPO.

How could $1 billion go missing? Or how could it not be visible one day, but very visible the next? The majority of the business world will say that there are plenty of reasons why Facebook (and others) pay so much for companies like Instagram: it's a calculation of the value of future business, or how much it's worth to keep these companies out of their competitors' hands. But that doesn't answer why the numbers are often so high or how they're calculated.

To us, this is the value of the relationships that Instagram had created. (We also know from statements that Facebook had made that it was interested in Instagram's users and didn't want Google, Apple, or someone else to get them.) It certainly wasn't Instagram's code. Google could have likely put a team of engineers on the project and in a few months created a very similar set of features that were also free to users. That would have cost them much less for the "same" thing (if all you were looking at were the features).

This isn't just the case for software and other technology companies. When Pixar was acquired by Disney in 2006, it was "worth" just under $2 billion, according to the company books, but "earned" an extra $2.3 billion in goodwill (an extra 100%). Nextel was "worth" $5.3 billion when it was purchased in 2004, but "earned" an extra $30 billion in goodwill (that's almost 680%!). Every healthy company, in every category, has premium value, but no one knows just how much until events like these. It's hidden from view by traditional business measures and blind to those who practice it.

It's fair to say that premium value is the largest component of relationship value (which comprises all five types of value). There's no traditional way to measure relationship value (or its premium component), but it would be foolish to claim it didn't exist.

And yet, the first two kinds of value, functional and financial, because they're relatively easy to measure, get most of the serious attention in business. Sometimes, as in the nonprofit world, or even in some places in government, they're not as stressed, but they're very visible. The other forms of value, the premium types, are also there, but blind spots cause companies to ignore them in a business setting, hand them off to people not accountable for the bottom line, or treat them as mercurial or random.

Because they've been difficult to define, articulate, and measure, some companies, such as ad agencies, have a tendency to lump the types of premium value together and call them *emotional*, because they're all equally invisible—unlike basic value, they take place on the inside, in people's states of mind. Branding firms do the same thing, but lump it all under *brand* (and, unfortunately, never differentiate the components). Regardless, they're distinct and need to be approached differently if you hope to innovate in order to grow premium value.

There is also a lack of effective tools for measuring and understanding premium value's impact on relationships. It's not enough to know it's there. Most business owners don't know how to visualize and understand this value, let alone relationships—and, less still, how to innovate to improve them. For them, these types of relationship values are equally significant blind spots. Most leaders know intuitively that these relationships are important and valuable, but they fail to prioritize or act on them when making either strategic or tactical decisions. Relationships don't show up on the income statement or on the balance sheet after the fact (in owner's equity). They don't make an appearance in strategic discussions, even though their long-term effect on both should be obvious. In fact, neither revenue nor profit is sustainable without the foundation that relationships provide.

At this point, we can't fully solve the "naming, defining, measuring" problem of premium value entirely, although Nathan and Steve gave it a shot in the book *Making Meaning: How Successful Businesses Deliver Meaningful Customer Experiences* (New Riders, 2006). Although there has been some progress in developing metrics, these forms of value have a certain intangibility (they exist only the mind, after all!) that will probably always make them tougher to work with quantitatively than the other, more basic forms of value. However, whereas relationships can't be easily measured, they can, in fact, be worked with to provide superior value for customers, to build superior returns for investors, and to build enduring relationships between businesses and customers that benefit both hugely.

A New Approach

This book offers a solution for building and managing relationships like these, one that's been deployed successfully in a wide range of contexts. It involves tools and processes that help you accomplish a number of tasks:

- Understanding and visualizing your relationships with customers
- Identifying the best opportunities for innovation (and total value)
- Creating better relationships

With these new tools and processes, you'll be able to see when and where your customers are having the experiences that create great relationships—and the value that comes with them (and when they're not). You'll learn how those customers feel when they first encounter your products or services. You'll understand how they feel when they buy them or if they regret buying them at all. You'll understand their reactions to your customer service and ongoing attempts to stay in contact with them. You'll also have a complete picture of where you interact with people, what happens when you do, and why it matters.

Knowing all this is not merely important in theory. It also provides a strategic foundation for innovating to improve relationships and increasing value for your company. You can turn from being passive and reactive to proactive and helpful. You'll be able to prioritize opportunities for improvement. You'll know where to innovate and what to expect from your efforts. And you'll be able to evaluate your innovation program over time. In other words, you'll understand and know how to influence your relationships, moving them from your blind spot into plain view.

You'll also begin to see the impact that your entire organization has on these relationships. They don't live in product development, customer service, or in the store. They live everywhere, because they're reinforced (or decreased) by nearly every action the company takes. This new view of relationships will give you a way to strategically tie together the disparate pieces of your organization and focus them on the impact they can have on building long-term value. Too often, one part of the organization is countering the gains of another part *because* there's no way to tie them together. Our tools help illuminate these at a strategic level and show how everyone within the organization can contribute to successful relationships (and more value).

At the beginning of this chapter, Comcast was painted in a fairly negative light; however, this company is trying to become more conscious of building lasting relationships. For example, it is creating online tools that enable people to do more for themselves—and thus avoid its harried service reps. This may seem to be an admission of failure, but it's actually a promising sign. The company is innovating to improve an experience that it knows isn't great. This is our goal, as well: to describe relationships so that you can innovate to make them better.

This book is divided into two halves. The first half, (Chapters 1–4), describes what relationships are and how they are built. It also introduces a tool called a *waveline diagram*. It provides a visual representation of relationships, since a picture is worth a thousand words and many more dollars. The second half (Chapters 5–12) looks at an innovation process called *becoming by doing*. It is a holistic program that touches not only on how to create things that your customers want, but also how to manage relationships inside and outside your company.

Welcome to the new world of relationships. Hopefully, this book will take them out of your blind spot and enable you to understand the value that relationships create for your company. As brand loyalty has fallen and customers have become both more fickle and more savvy, it's time to start focusing on their real needs and consciously build a relationship with them.

EYE OPENERS

In this chapter, we've introduced a new definition of value in business (and design) and how it requires us to take a new approach to designing and developing much improved customer relationships. To recap what we've said:

- There are five kinds of value that get exchanged between people, and these are always potentials in any relationship: functional, financial, emotional, identity, and meaningful.

- The types of value that are easily measured quantitatively (functional and financial) are well understood and attended to in business because they are much easier to assess and plan for.

- The three types of value that are more elusive in nature (emotional, identity, and meaningful) are more difficult to measure and plan for, which is why they aren't typically a part of product development or customer relationship planning. This leads to missed opportunities to provide higher levels of value to customers.

- These more premium types of value often have a much bigger financial impact than the more basic types of value.

- Value can't be exchanged without a relationship of some kind, making the design of customer relationships central to the realization of any business value be they basic or premium.

- Relationships don't occur outside of some kind of experience, making the design of the customer experience, over time, central to long-term business value, as well.

- We need new, improved business tools to help develop better relationships and more premium value from these understandings, but it's already clear that traditional tools are inadequate in keeping businesses focused on premium value.

2

Defining a Business Relationship

Sisters Alexandra and Isabella, 5 and 7, are heading to their first encounter with Disneyland. They've watched Disney movies their entire lives, but they haven't been completely engulfed by the Disney experience.

Their anticipation is high, but they really don't know what to expect. Their father and grandmother have told them stories about their own trips to Disneyland when they were young (this will be a three-generational experience), and they know it's a place, but they truly aren't prepared for what they will encounter.

Their first morning, they're abuzz as if it were Christmas. They know that they will have breakfast with a princess and, hopefully, get her autograph. When they finally cross the looooooong parking *lot and get to the park entrance, they are already entranced and nearly speechless—nearly.*

They can see the Magic Castle far in the distance. They practically run through the gate to the statue of Mickey. They almost forget about the princess breakfast as their senses are already on overload. The castle pulls them forward, but they are overwhelmed by all the exciting things to see, stop, and investigate as they walk down Main Street.

When they finally encounter a character, she is the evil queen from Snow White and the Seven Dwarves. *They are simultaneously excited and scared, but they get her autograph and speak with her about their first-ever visit.*

Later, after many rides, something to eat, finally meeting Mickey (as well as two different princesses), they are speaking with one of the dwarves when the evil queen emerges from around a corner. With the dwarf, they hide in the bushes, but the queen finds them and immediately addresses them by name: "Ali! Bella! I thought you were on MY side!" They are amazed that the queen remembered them and scared that they might have to make a choice: stay and talk with the dwarf or join the queen. It's a lot to take in for five- and seven-year-old girls.

Years later, they will likely take their own children to Disneyland in much the same way, presaging some of what their children will experience, reminiscing about this very trip. They may not remember the experience as it actually happened, but, instead will embellish it in the retelling and the remembering.

The first step toward making the most of relationships is to know exactly what they are and how you can affect them. In business, a relationship is a connection forged over time by interactions between a person and a company that provides lasting value for both parties. Every interaction, from a sales call to the ongoing use of a product, can build toward a good or bad relationship.

In this chapter, you'll look at the building blocks of relationships, the opportunities for making them better, and how you can use them strategically to build value over time.

The Best Relationships in the World

Start by celebrating a company that probably gets relationships better than any other. If you have small children, you're likely familiar with Disney. First, your kids fell in love with the movies. Then your shelves filled up with Disney books. Your kids may even have a favorite character and imagine it to be real.

Then one day you take your kids to Disneyland, which is no small investment. A single day for a family of four costs almost $400, not including extras, and there are always extras. But as you walk through the gates, you immediately know it's worth it. Disneyland delivers on every promise. There are real castles and real characters. Mickey Mouse is there, and you never see two Mickeys at the same time (which reinforces the faux reality). There are rides and parades and a massive world to explore.

As a parent, you begin to notice something else, too. Disneyland has been designed by people whose attention to detail borders on the insane. You can't find a single corner of the park, no matter how obscure, where someone hasn't thought about the toadstools or the trash cans. Not only that, but Disneyland even has many hidden treasures that you can encounter only if you look in the most unlikely places. Here's a very short sampling of the hundreds of extras in the park:

- The park is filled with hidden images of Mickey Mouse. You'll find them stamped in concrete and barely visible on the ceilings of rides. Some of the lighting is designed so that objects throw Mickey-shaped shadows.

- In Cinderella's castle, if you look overhead, you can find the mice from the movie peeking out from the rafters.

- The Haunted Mansion is filled with hidden surprises. For example, when you get off the elevator, there is a room that looks like an office off to one side. You're not supposed to go over there, but if you do, you'll see that the book on the desk is a dictionary opened to the word "death."

- If you pick up the vintage phone next to the Candy Store on Main Street, you'll hear a conversation between a woman and her daughter about what they should buy.
- If you linger in the parking lot, you can get a goodnight kiss from the castle 30 minutes after the park closes.

This all may seem obsessive, but it's necessary. Disney has to be magical for the kids who visit it (and, possibly, the adults, too), no matter what they do or how they explore the park. Of course, everyone takes a different path and has different experiences each time they go. You might take a wrong turn and end up in an unlikely place. Or your kid picks up a phone she shouldn't have. To fill your child with wonder, even the most unlikely interactions have to be perfect and potentially filled with *wonder*. Disney understands this.

So, Disney gets relationships. It creates a delightful number of places infused with wonder. It doesn't rest. It always delivers. And the company gets a reward, too. It can charge far more for a visit than any other theme park. Its visitors also tend to come for a few days in a row to make sure they haven't missed anything. Good relationships build value. They really do.

Relationships with Organizations

At this point, you may object that what we're describing is not, in fact, a *relationship*, because relationships can exist only between people. Some may also object that this discussion is reminiscent of the recent, questionable Supreme Court decision reiterating that, in legal terms, corporations are, essentially, the same as people.

Let's put the "corporations are people" objection to rest first and agree that an organization formed by people is *not* the same thing as a single person. For one thing, an organization has no corporeal presence in the world. For another, it has no autonomous consciousness. Perhaps, in the future, other, non-physical creations of people, like artificial intelligences, may prompt reconsideration. But, for now, let's agree that a corporation is *not* a person.

That leaves the primary objection: that people can't really have a relationship with an organization (and vice versa). There's really no reason to make such an assertion. As the Merriam-Webster Dictionary describes it, a relationship is "the way in which two or more people, groups, countries, etc., talk to, behave toward, and deal with each other." Clearly, people can talk to, behave toward, and deal with companies.

People also react to what companies do and often imagine companies *as if* they were people. In fact, as stated in the introduction to this book, there is ample evidence that people do just this. In addition, corporations are often sufficiently aware of this personification tendency that they seek to influence, imagining their companies as having characters and creating personas that align with the sort of personality customers may want them to have.[1]

It's possible that underlying these objections may be a general uneasiness with the current state of people-to-people relationships and a fear that individuals may confuse the relationships they develop with companies as worthy substitutes for the real thing. This is exactly the conversation that occurs continuously in regard to technology's impact on society.

Ultimately, because humans are social beings (and busy ones at that), they must develop and maintain valued relationships to survive and thrive. And it's difficult to imagine a situation in which people-to-organization relationships would provide enough of what we need as social beings to result in healthy, thriving individuals. That said, because people tend to personify organizations as well as value people-to-company relationships that provide great experiences, there is no reason to fear the development and evolution of such relationships. They augment other social relationships, often resulting in richer lives

---

1. Added Value, a market insights firm where one of the authors worked, has specialized in creating such personas.

for all concerned. They also serve as an important metaphor for seeing how we relate to each other.

In the final chapter of this book, we muse a bit about whether great people-to-company relationships may actually enhance people's capacities to have great people-to-people relationships. For now, though, let's simply work with the reality that people value relationships with certain companies, under certain circumstances, and by working to evoke those relationships they can make customers' lives better.

What Makes a Relationship

Thankfully, not every company needs to be as experience-obsessed as Disney. But your company is in the relationship business, whether you like it or not. People will develop a positive feeling about your company or not. They can be wholly indifferent to you, or love you to the point that they won't go anywhere else. You can drive value with relationships, or you can ignore both the relationships and the value that comes with them. And, if you aren't working toward creating a positive relationship, you're most likely creating a negative one.

Here is how relationships work:

- **Relationships are a connection.** If you think of how a child feels about Disney, the word "love" jumps to the forefront. In fact, if you think of your favorite brands, you'll see that you probably care deeply about them because these companies have provided customers with experiences that mattered to them. If you were amazed in a good way by your iPhone 4 and 5, you'll probably spend money again for an iPhone 6.

- **Relationships are based on experiences that people value.** In the corporate world, the word *experience* describes everything from websites to ceiling fans. Experiences are critical because that's where relationships occur. So they need to be carefully designed. However, focusing on experiences without considering the relationships they enable is short-sighted and can lead companies down a path that doesn't fulfill their strategies.

For relationship innovation, imagine how people experience things. What happens when you interact with a phone or toy? Do you value that experience? Sometimes the answer is *yes*; for example, your child has a valued experience when she's amazed by Disneyland. Other times the answer is *no*, such as a negative experience when you argue with a customer service representative. Often, you don't have much of an experience at all when reading a web page while looking for information—but you could.

Valued experiences typically change your state of mind—hopefully for the better. When you feel that a particular shirt makes you look good, it gives you confidence. When your exclusive platinum credit card makes you feel successful, that's a valued experience.

- **Relationships are created over time.** Think again about a shirt that you love. Of course, because you love it, you'll probably order a few more items from the same company. They may also turn out to be satisfying and give you that same level of confidence. You're hoping that magic will strike again. This, too, is a valued experience. As a result, if they continue to deliver what you like and expect, you start to feel a deeper connection with the company. You stay with them as they change to stay in fashion, and you become partners in an ongoing social journey.

- **Not everyone experiences a company the same way, but that doesn't matter.** No two people or interactions are exactly alike, but people's overall experiences can be remarkably similar over time. Disneyland knows that everyone is going to take his or her own path through its parks—they design for that—but it will largely be similar from an experience standpoint. Businesses need to realize that while they cannot plan exactly how people interact with their products and services, they can work to make sure that key interactions produce great experiences.

- **Finally, relationships are strategic, and they involve a long time frame.** Their purpose is not to create quick sales, but to make your products or services more valuable to people over time. As a result, consider relationships as a long-term investment. Disney could easily skimp on paint and maintenance and save a good deal of money. Its investors have occasionally asked for exactly that. But that would destroy the magic, which would lessen the experience and, ultimately, the relationship. Over the

CASE STUDY: HOW COCA COLA BUILDS VALUE

During the American Super Bowl in 1979, viewers were treated to what's become known as one of the greatest ads of all time: "Hey kid, catch." It starred football player "Mean" Joe Greene and a young boy. As a player, Greene was known for living up to his nickname: he was tough and mean. Early in his career, he physically assaulted opposing players and screamed at his teammates when they made mistakes. But the commercial turned his reputation on its head. In it, he was shown coming in exhausted from a game. A kid steps out and hands him a Coke. Greene drinks it down in one gulp and turns to limp away. The boy now looks crestfallen. His hero has not only ignored him but also drunk his Coke. As he turns away, he hears Greene say, "Hey kid, catch." When he looks back at Greene, the player tosses his football jersey to him.

The ad is amazingly touching. Even if you're not a Coke fan, it delivers a great feeling, or a valued experience. It touches you and makes you feel something. The Coca-Cola Company is one of the best in the world at doing this. Although its products are nearly identical to others in function and price, its ability to make people smile is something that makes us care about the company.

Not convinced? Let's look at a unique promotion the company did several years ago for Friendship Day in Latin America. Friendship day is a big holiday in that region. Typically, people spend it with their best friend. That day, Coke debuted a unique Friendship Machine (see figure opposite).

long haul, this approach destroys the very possibility for the relationship, itself, creating a much bigger problem in the long term.

In fact, the biggest obstruction to building relationships is a business's need to focus on the short term. With quarterly numbers always around the corner, you'll often find companies trying to bump up sales through gimmicks, without investing in long-term value. At the end of the day, you have to decide whether you want to sell Coke or generic soda. And that shouldn't be a hard decision.

It was three meters high, and the coin slot was high above a person's head. The kicker was that if two people worked together to get a soda, the machine rewarded them with two for the price of one. People loved it and posted thousands of videos of friends helping each other, often laughing, to get a free drink. By providing such experiences over time, Coke has built a vast and loyal following. It has great relationships with its customers, who are happy to pay a premium to buy its products.

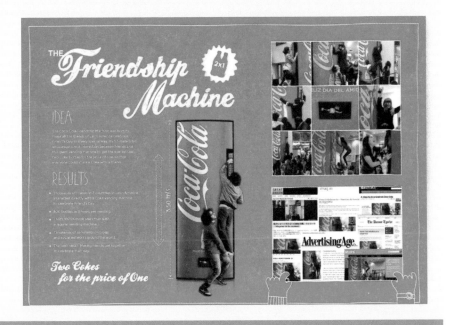

DIMENSIONS OF AN EXPERIENCE

What separates an ordinary, single interaction, like receiving a bill, from a valued experience? Research has found that experiences typically work in six dimensions: value, consistency, intensity, duration, triggers, and interaction.

Value. On what levels does your experience (and relationship) provide and exchange value? Are you offering functional value for financial value? Are you engaging on a level of emotional value or triggering someone's sense of identity? If you're connecting with your customer's core meanings, you're providing the deepest value possible and customers are usually more willing to pay more, in return. Some companies are successful playing at the most surface levels while companies that reap the highest rewards operate at the deepest.

Consistency. Experiences only work over time if they seem to come from the same place. Whenever a customer interacts with your company, no matter what the touchpoint, it must feel consistent. If your advertising promises one thing but your product delivers another, you look forced or fake, just as inconsistent people seem dishonest and untrustworthy—or at least, unprofessional.

The trick, here, is that the experience should be consistent in human terms, not in absolute, engineering terms. Technically, this may make them seem inconsistent, but as long as they follow your customers' expectations they will feel natural. For example, just because customers might expect to find one of your products in different places doesn't pose a problem that all of your products aren't also (consistently) in more than one place. Or just because some of your experiences are different in person than online (while others aren't), doesn't mean they're wrong if it's how customers think they should be.

Intensity. Intensity involves how much the touchpoint resonates in someone's mind. Some interactions are so low-key that they impact a user about as much as brushing their teeth. But most valued experiences have intensity. They have the power to captivate and change you. An adult's experience of a NASCAR race should be as exciting and dynamic as it can be. A pair of shoes can make you feel terrific, and a blender can make you happy if it makes the perfect margarita—or makes it effortlessly. But your experience needs to be reasonably intense to be valued.

Sometimes, of course, customers don't want a particular interaction to be intense at all. Or they want to relax. Finding the proper intensity for a touchpoint is an important part of improving the experiences people will have.

Duration. Duration is just what it says: how long an interaction lasts. Obviously, you want the wait for a customer service call to be as short as possible. You'd like a spa treatment to be much longer. Managing these intervals is as important as any other part of the interaction—for example, taking the right amount of time and making the transitions in and out of the experience smooth. More important is your understanding of *when* the interaction actually starts. (Hint: it's much earlier than you likely think.)

sidebar continues on next page

Triggers. Triggers involve how people react to different design elements within touchpoints. Every element of an interaction can evoke different responses in people. You may love bamboo because it's a hard, environmentally responsible material, but some of your customers may think of it as a cheap artifact of the 1960s. You may like earth tones, but your customer may associate them with dirt. All of your design decisions trigger responses in people, and you have to be certain of what these are before you deploy them. You don't get to define the reactions. The best you can hope for is to uncover and design to them.

Interaction. *Interaction* commonly refers to *interactive media*; this definition is a little shortsighted. Whenever a business creates a touchpoint, it can choose how it interacts with customers—as passive objects, or responding to their actions like a skilled concierge. More and more, people expect the latter—though not everywhere. They want intelligent products and personal interactions that anticipate their needs and treat them appropriately.

How Customers Interact with Companies' Touchpoints

On the other side of the universe from Disney is almost any Department of Motor Vehicles (DMV) in the United States. A visit to the DMV is universally dreaded. Typically, you arrive to a roomful of loud people and have to stand in line based on the DMV's own bureaucratic categories, which make no sense to anyone who doesn't work there. Is a motorcycle license the same as a driver's license? Do you need a Marine Class 1 or Marine Class 2 boating permit? What if you just want an ID card and don't plan to drive at all? Very few people know how the DMV categorizes these needs, and, as a result, they often wait too long in one line only to be told they need to go to a different one. Then, when they finally get to the right place, they are shunted through a confusing process of tests and paperwork. They have little understanding of what's going on or where the endpoint is, and their only hope is to somehow emerge with the document they need.

Unlike Disney, the DMV doesn't seem to care much about your experience (and, therefore, you). If you hate it, so what? You like driving, don't you? The DMV seems to only care about itself and its own way of working. It wants to frog march as many people as it can as quickly as possible through its own processes. As a result, it gives customers no ability to affect how they're being treated. They can endure it or leave.

Because they don't have competition, the DMV doesn't *have* to care about relationships. And, because they aren't seen as a source of value, there's no incentive to improve the experience beyond lessening their own costs. Few businesses, however, are in that position. Most face stiff competition, either from direct competitors or indirect ones (like workarounds). Comcast may have a particular territory locked-up as the exclusive cable provider, but it still faces competition from satellite TV and even piracy.

The DMV and Disney show the range of interactions you can have with a company. When your child chats with a Disneyland character, the interaction is free-flowing. The character improvises on the spot to reflect whatever your child is saying and doing. By contrast, the DMV insists that you do exactly as it says, regardless of what you need or how you respond. There is seldom room for deviation, special circumstances, or even a modicum of graciousness.

Design experts typically specify three major types of interactions you can have with a company: top-down, co-created, and improvised. Of course, many experiences can straddle or fall between them, but for simplicity's sake, look at them one at a time.

POTENTIAL TOUCHPOINTS

Organizations connect with their customers (or governments with their constituents) in many ways. There are many kinds of touchpoints where the relationship is created and reinforced or starts to fail. Most organizations don't plan for a complete list, don't pay attention to many important ones, or never synchronize between them, which negates the power of each. Often, this is because touchpoints are the responsibility of different divisions—or even outside organizations. As such, the organization's strategy doesn't include them all, leaving gaps and blind spots in the relationship. Here is a (mostly) complete list of the kinds of touchpoints that most organizations create. All are potential points in which the relationship can be grown or destroyed:

- Physical products
- Telephone (including support call centers, office answering services, recordings, and voicemail systems)
- In-person service people (such as cashiers, waiters, concierges, and managers)
- Business cards
- Correspondence (including letterhead, envelopes, and so on)
- Social media accounts, tweets, posts, blogs, and so on
- Physical locations (such as stores, kiosks, service centers, headquarters, showrooms, and so on)
- Packaging and labeling
- Advertisements (such as magazine, in-store, billboards, in-air, mailers, product placement, TV, and so on)
- Websites and online venues
- Television and radio (programming, ads, sponsorship, and inadvertent mentions, and so on)
- Signage
- Events

Top-Down

In this kind of interaction, the company doesn't give you any choice in how things go. From the DMV example, you might think this is always a bad idea, but that's not necessarily the case. When you're watching a movie, you don't want anyone asking your opinion on the climax. If you go to a symphony, you don't want the conductor to ask if you want to step in on the oboe or if you'd like more timpani. Few choose-your-own-adventure books end with the same sense of drama and dénouement, at least for adults. You almost always have a much better experience of a concert, film, or book if you turn the control over to a master.

Many times, a company has no choice except to make a particular touchpoint top-down. Every digital storefront, for example, needs a shopping cart and checkout process. The customer has no say in creating or designing that interaction. Most of the time, this interaction doesn't result in a valued experience. But it can also affect you in a good or bad way. The Apple Store, for example, already had a great purchase process when it, like most retailers, stored your credit card information and required only a password for you to buy something. Then it added Apple Pay and a pay-by-fingerprint feature, and the resulting interaction became (for a time) remarkable.

Co-Created

In a co-created interaction, you and the organization both bring something to the table. Wikipedia is a great example of this, where users actually create the content and Wikipedia serves as a facilitator. Reddit is another example: individuals post and edit content, whereas the site merely facilitates the interaction and selects the moderators. One of the easiest ways to create a valuable relationship is to allow people, where appropriate, to contribute to its creation. We simply care more about the things we invest our own time in.

You can also find an ambiguous middle ground between top-down and co-created. The Android operating system allows for a lot of customization. You can greatly affect how it interacts with you, but there are always rules and limits to what you can do. Some Levi's stores have a machine that takes your measurements and then lets you specify how the pants flare out, their color, and so on. Still, it eventually makes a pair of pants, not a fruit salad. In this case, Levi's is enabling customization but not full-on co-creation. It's an invitation to customers to work within parameters but not one to do whatever they want (or to ask for things that aren't possible).

For example, consider an unusual art gallery, the now-closed Feature Gallery in New York.

In an interview for this book, its late owner, Hudson (he went by one name), described how curators typically design visitor experiences. They usually organize galleries so that people see the least impressive work first and most expensive and famous at the end. In other words, they create a building narrative that rises to a climax.

You might wonder how this is possible if a museum has an open path that allows people to walk wherever they want (as opposed to some exhibits that have only one path through). After all, if visitors have choice and control, how can anyone shape those choices and paths? This is an important concept in building relationships with customers. Overall, people are remarkably predictable, and most will have the same experiences from your offerings. Most people who enter supermarkets shop for produce first. Most people who browse a website do so in similar patterns, so much so that companies have developed algorithms that can predict, with reasonable accuracy) what you will need or do next, whether or not you're in a hurry, or when to offer customer service. There's nothing wrong with this kind of responsiveness and customization. Indeed, if it weren't the case, we would be much more frustrated, and companies would have to develop separate paths for each person in order to serve them comfortably. These typical responses to choices and stimuli are what allow all of us (museum curators and web designers, alike) to design satisfying experiences for more than one person (see the section on triggers in Chapter 7, "Discovering").

In the case of art galleries, it turns out that almost all people turn right when they enter. Although some stray from the path, the vast majority will walk through a gallery in exactly the same pattern. That allows curators to draw them through an experience that unfolds much like a narrative, even though everyone officially has permission to go where they like. Typically, a museum or gallery uses this fact to build a predictable narrative based on a chronology of the artist's works: early works in the front, later works at the end.

However, Hudson believed that this approach belonged in the past. Instead, each visitor should not only be able to improvise his or her experience, but also be encouraged to do so. To make this a reality, he didn't use the usual organizational principles in his gallery. Instead, he broke conventions, juxtaposed works in new ways, and organized the gallery space to lead the visitor in unusual directions. In this way, Feature disrupted everyone's expectations and delivered fresh experiences that forced them to concentrate much more on the work than they would have done otherwise. The organization of an experience changes how easily different stories can be told or discovered. If you want to tell a unique story about yourselves, your organization, or its offerings, you can't expect to do so in the same format that everyone uses.

And lest you think this led to its downfall, it didn't. Feature was an iconic gallery that introduced many famous artists to the world. It closed simply because Hudson died, and it was too difficult for others to replicate his vision and process.

Improvised

In improvised situations, the company responds directly to what a customer says or does in a freeform way. This type of interaction offers a much more human sense of give and take. That's why improvised interactions offer the greatest potential for success and, needless to say, for failure.

Starwood Hotels, for example, treats its best customers to a concierge service. This is a single person whose phone number you have. You can call that person whenever you like, even if you're just in the planning stages of your trip. Your special person helps you with whatever unique needs you have, hopefully producing a valued experience. The things she suggests you do on the road also can help you have a great experience. Most importantly, however, she gets to know you over time and can serve you better as the relationship continues. Such a service is improvised because it responds to your unique inputs and grows in its ability to help you.

Improvisation has a long history within various kinds of storytelling, especially in music and theater. The principles that jazz musicians and improvisational actors use may go by different titles but share important similarities:

- **Accept all offers** (an offer is a prompt or action on the part of one character). Denying an offer by ignoring it kills game play and creates an unresponsive experience. Accepting an offer moves the story forward collaboratively.

- **Rather than trying to devise an offer, assume one has already been made** (by a customer's actions or an event in the environment). Act on those offers. In other words, don't wait for your customers to do something or be explicit about their desires; engage them proactively.

- **Use what's already there.** Rather than specifically creating new material that may be erroneous or take too much time, use what's already present in the experience and relationships. Allow customers to use their own material (information, preferences, ideas, and so on), but be ready with suggestions if they get stuck.

Improvisation is a good analogy for how many customer experiences unfold, and it's especially important in digital media (though more difficult to accomplish). If there isn't a person guiding the experience (like a salesperson or customer support agent), the system should improvise and provide a coherent experience, automatically, no matter what the customer does. This provides more value than a static experience that is the same for everyone, regardless of what they do, but it requires much more thought, planning, and engineering. However, if you value the best experiences, websites and online services must do this, regardless of the complexity. Games do this, inherently, as the experience unfolds for a user despite the variations in behavior that she may exhibit (not to mention her goals). This kind of system behavior creates an experience that goes far beyond mere tasks, and it enables both the reaction to and the expression of emotions, values, and core meanings by customers and audiences (and influence over the customer's state of mind).

Which type of interaction you have or choose is up to you. The important thing is to have the right interaction, to evoke the right experience, for the right person, at the right time because you considered it, not because others have done it or it's a default.

Customer Time Versus Corporate Time

The next step in understanding a relationship is to see what happens to customers as they connect with touchpoints over time. Remember: a single wonderful experience is not enough. You have to make sure your customers have many valued experiences over time to keep the relationship going and that these different touchpoints reinforce each other, collectively. To do this, experiences must happen on your customers' preferred time frame.

Many businesses have this figured out. Hotel services are usually arranged around their customer's schedule, rather than what would be best for them. If the hotel had its way, the most efficient path would be to have visitors up, fed, and out the door as early as possible. That way, its housekeepers could come in all at once, in one shift, and do their thing. But the customer may not want that, which is why housekeepers linger with little to do in the early morning. Similarly, it would be best for a fine dining restaurant to get through as many customers as possible in a short time. Instead, they move at their customers' more leisurely pace. This highlights two ways to organize an experience through time.

- **Corporate time.** The schedule on which companies can efficiently produce and deliver products, services, events, and promotions.
- **Customer time.** The continuous engagement customers have with the world as they interact with a company. In other words, they live in the world and that drives the pace they want.

The biggest difference between the two is that customer time isn't only focused on one organization's products and services in a vacuum. For customers, time flows along in their lives as they interact with everyone's products and services (not just one company's). Designing experiences from the customer's perspective needs to take into account a much wider set of events. Corporate time usually lurches forward on its internal schedule and only takes into account what happens in the organization. There are campaign launches, product drops, important trade shows, ad schedules, and so on, many of which have nothing to do with what customers want.

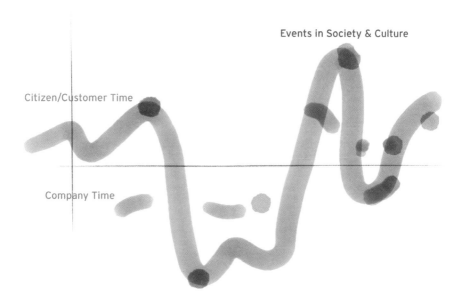

Events in Society & Culture

Citizen/Customer Time

Company Time

A great example of this is how many technology companies approach the release of new versions of their products. A vice president at an enterprise software company tells of the dynamic within his company that governs product releases. He explained how customers aren't interested in frequent releases to the products they use; in fact, customers *don't* want their products to change often. So, their tolerance for change is low, as are their expectations of the need for change. However, the leadership within the company is highly concerned about losing great salespeople who look for the opportunity to resell software in order to earn their commissions and keep their jobs lucrative and interesting. Two years is about all they'll wait for a major update that allows them to resell to their past customers. In this case, corporate time calls for a release every two years, whereas customer time wants something much more gradual. The two are in marked conflict, and which path the company chooses says something about its relationship priorities.

It's important to understand and be sensitive to customer time. You can't merely look at moments when you reach out to your customers. You have to look at what happens at all times. Your customers don't just live in your world. They have touchpoints with your competitors, partners, each other, and a myriad of other sources. They live in a world that is much bigger than yours, so you should take account of at least *some* of these other interactions if you hope to build a successful relationship with them. That doesn't mean you must interact with them all of the time—in fact, you want to stay out of the way when you're not wanted. But you do need to take their mindsets into account, interact when they want you to, and make them feel better if you can. Remember after 9/11 when movie studios pulled their release schedules for violent films or stalled comedy programs until people were in better moods (or bigger need) to laugh? Those actions were responding to customer time instead of corporate time.

Above all, you should not put customers on corporate time if you can avoid it because it has nothing to do with their lives. They may put up with it, but they won't love it.

The Pace of Change

The pace of a relationship tells you how often a customer wants to experience your company or a change in their circumstances. To understand it, you should recognize a few principles:

- **Understand that your relationship time frame may be much longer than you think.** Too many companies view the relationship boundaries as starting and stopping with the touchpoint or even the transaction. Relationships, however, start earlier and last longer than any touchpoint or transaction, and any development must stretch over this longer period in order to be effective. You can't neglect any part of the relationship, although you may want to focus on some interactions more than others.

- **You should only interact when needed.** Nobody wants to hear from you all of the time. Apple renews its operating system every year or so, adding new features and capabilities that make its customers happy. But it doesn't do it every day, because it would annoy most of its users to learn a new interface more often. Theoretically, you could send your customers a great offer every day, but you'd be foolish to do so.

- **And don't forget, you're interacting any time a customer uses your product.** If you sell garden tools, the best thing you can do is make sure they are produced well and renew your relationship every time they are used. As a result, not much further interaction is necessary.

- **Relationships go through phases.** The intensity of your interaction with your customers will change over time. It's important to keep it up, and to know when you should reach out and feed the relationship. If you think about a company that makes watches, it does not need to contact its customers often. But after a while, customers tire of the experience their watches provide, so the company should be ready to intervene and make the relationship evolve.

Setting the Tone

So there's good news and bad news. The good news is that it's not difficult to understand how you're doing over time. Everyone has personal relationships, and that makes it easy to understand how companies can build relationships as well. You can figure out how to improve relationships and devise steps for doing so. You simply have to take an active role in researching and understanding what's wanted and do your best to fulfill that.

The following are a few core principles that you should observe:

- **Not all relationships are meant to be.** Frankly, you can't please everyone all of the time. You merely want to structure experiences so that you build strong valuable relationships with as many customers as possible or with the ones that are most valuable to you.

- **The best relationships thrive on clear communication.** As with personal relationships, the best way to manage a relationship is to always be transparent and clear. You have to be real. It's no longer enough to appear as if a company has certain ideals or values. Social media has made it nearly impossible to hide who you are. It's dead simple these days for customers to call you out on your own behavior.

- **In addition to stating your values, you now have to live them.** This isn't to say that every person in a corporation has to be a clone, but if they aren't at least aligned with the organization's goals and values, they may eventually be at odds with its mission. Front-line employees, such as wait staff and customer-service representatives, have to be especially vigilant. They can quickly make apparent a mismatch of values and kill any customer affinity that could develop into a good relationship.

The Problem of Habituation

Think back a few weeks about what music you were listening to. There was probably a song that, when it came on the radio, made you stop talking and raise the volume. It made you feel better immediately and took you on a great emotional journey.

Today, the song doesn't affect you that way. It comes on the radio, and you won't turn it up. It may do little for you now. This is known as *habituation*. As you do something or use something more frequently, typically, the intensity of your reactions falls over time. You probably love your car the moment you buy it. Four months later, however, it's not so special, and a year later, you may barely notice it. Habituation is a central challenge in building relationships with people. Over time, your clients can overlook you if you're not renewing the relationship and providing them with new, positive feelings. And that's a shame because digital media has made it much easier to reach people, even if it's also increased the number of voices competing for their attention. Responding to habituation requires constant adjustment of touch-points, while taking into account the pace of change that customers will prefer. It can be a difficult balancing act, but an essential one.

Relationships as a Strategy

Take a look at one final example to understand the long-term importance of relationship thinking. In 2006, Porsche released a brilliant commercial in which a young boy saw a new sports car from his classroom window). He was so entranced that he failed to listen to his teacher, much to his embarrassment. However, after school, he rode his bike over to a Porsche dealership. The salesman was surprised at first, but let the boy sit in the car. In the end, he asked the boy, "What do you think?"

The kid replied, "I'll see you in 20 years."

Whether Porsche lives up to that promise or not, at least the company recognized that relationships are a strategic opportunity. They involve long-term thinking and a clear view of everything involved with their customer interactions. In the commercial, Porsche argued that it takes an extraordinarily long view of customer relationships. It realizes that the relationship doesn't start the moment a customer walks into the dealership; rather, it can start years before, develop over time, and last years after purchase. The story may be cute, but the message is critical.

Relationship innovation has a deep and important goal: making a meaningful connection that transcends what your products and services do. You should never confuse this goal with building customer loyalty. Although good relationships do produce loyal customers, you can also have loyal customers without a good relationship. Any company that offers discounts can gain some measure of loyalty. But it's a shallow, spurious loyalty. If another company discounts deeper or if your customer moves up in income, you could easily lose your customer. You're not loyal if you cheat at the first opportunity. You are loyal if your interactions with a company transcend challenges, and this only happens when relationships are meaningful and valuable to you.

The lynchpin in all of this is that you need a full view of all of your activities to make sense of them. You have to see how you're supporting or disappointing your customers over time—and where your best opportunities lie for innovation. The next chapter looks at the *waveline diagram*, a tool that gives you a full view of how a customer sees, understands, and experiences your company's products and services.

EYE OPENERS

This chapter shows how people build relationships with companies over time. Customers enter into a series of interactions, some of which have the potential to produce valued and meaningful experiences. If you can create such experiences over time, and your rhythm of expectation works, you can create a durable long-term relationship.

Here are a few ideas that hopefully will spark a conversation about relationship innovation.

- How many different parts of your company create different kinds of interactions through different touchpoints?
- How are you coordinating those efforts?
- To what extent are you providing consistent messaging or a consistent voice over time? Does your organization have a holistic "personality," or do you present a mish-mash of different, disconnected experiences?
- What kinds of touchpoints are you creating?
- Can you tell if you are triggering the right experiences, or are you providing top-down ones when a co-created or improvised interaction would be better?
- How often do people interact with your business?
- To what extent are you oriented to your customers' time frame versus only your own?
- Are you reaching out too much or too little—or just the right amount?
- Are you being real with them? How can you tell?
- How closely are you living your organization's values? If not, what are you doing to mitigate the risk of losing your customers' relationships once they find out?
- To what extent are you using the improvement of your customers' experiences as a strategic tool to building long-term value?

3

Visualizing Relationships

In the previous chapter, you learned how relationships can be created or destroyed by the way a customer experiences your brand and products over time. Theory is great, but you also need a framework for taking action to build and improve those relationships.

This chapter introduces the waveline diagram, a visual tool for building and improving relationships. It can deliver a snapshot of any touchpoint or the relationship as a whole. By enabling you to see exactly the experiences and value you're providing your customers, you can quickly identify areas for improvement and find surprising new places for innovation.

Oddly enough, this tool originally came from the world of music. Musicians have long been expert at shaping their audience's experience over time—and brands and businesses can learn a lot from them.

The Forgotten Composer

The life of Ernst Toch reflects the nature of ambition. Born in the Austro-Hungarian Empire in 1887, he trained himself to write music. Unfortunately, his parents weren't in favor of such a career, so he went to the University of Vienna to study medicine. He continued to write in his spare time, and in 1909, he stunned the music world by winning the Mozart Prize, which is given every four years to only one young composer. The idea that an untrained amateur could win such a prestigious contest made him an instant sensation. Soon after, Toch abandoned his medical studies and launched a career in music.

During the 1920s, his works were celebrated and sought after by the world's foremost conductors and most discerning concertgoers. But that was not to last. Like many Jewish musicians, his career was disrupted by the rise of Nazi Germany, and in 1934 he fled to America. He got a job at USC and started working for Hollywood. His film scores were nominated for three Academy Awards, but his more serious composition career faltered, and he had trouble getting his works performed. Disappointed, he eventually came to label himself "the forgotten composer."

Toch did, however, find lasting recognition in another way. In 1948, he published a book called *The Shaping Forces in Music*. It quickly became a classic instructional text for composers and is still in wide use today.

You might wonder why a book about musical composition would be interesting in a business context. Of course, it's not because of music, per se. It's because of a tool he developed to express its effect: *the waveline* (see figure). In music, it traces the intensity of the audience's emotions over time.

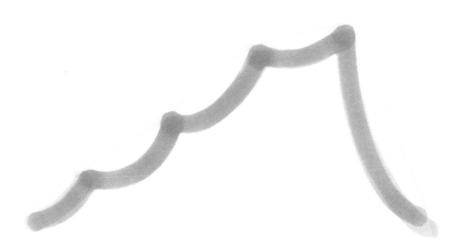

The good news is that wavelines do not need to be restricted to music or even to emotional journeys. With a few important adjustments, you can use them to describe almost any experience. They can trace the reactions of someone watching a movie, getting married, or hiking up a challenging mountain. They can also track the intensity of a person's interactions with a company.

Introduction to a Waveline Diagram

As you can see in the following figure, Steve's company, Scansion, has elaborated on Toch's waveline. This waveline charts the experience of a person shopping for and then using a tablet PC over several months, and it consists of several elements:

1. A timeline across the bottom that indicates how the sequences of experiences unfold, as well as how touchpoints are used to make that happen.

2. Phases of engagement marked across the top from initial to final interaction.

3. A Y-axis that charts intensity of experience (from positive to negative).

4. The important touchpoints where customers interact with an organization.

5. The experience a person has before and after each touchpoint.

6. A waveline that describes each customer segment's current experience.

7. An ideal waveline that describes the customer's desired experience (the one at the top).

Consumer Experience Waveline

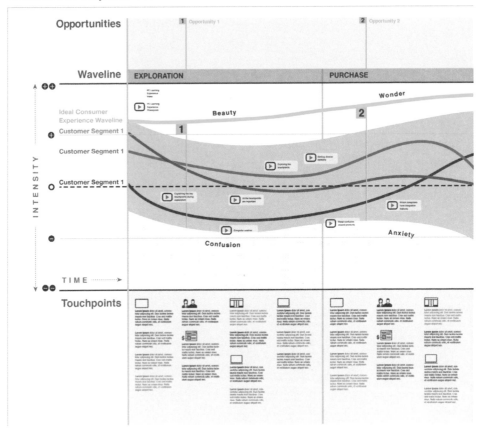

8. Opportunities called out on the bottom, which correspond to where and how the waveline can be improved.

9. The waveline diagram populated with evidence from the Discovery phase of work that, for example, can show videos of customers' own words that bolster conclusions at any point in the waveline.

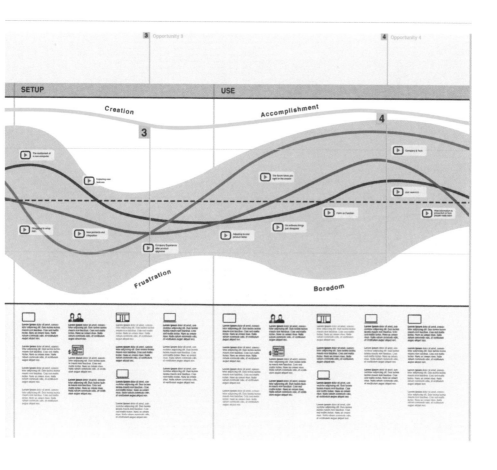

To understand a waveline diagram, contrast it with a common and useful tool that many companies employ today: a customer *journey map*. Typically, this is a linear map that lists every touchpoint between the brand, service, or product and customer, as well as what a customer thinks or needs at that moment. The idea is to ensure that needs are met, and the customer is never overwhelmed with too much interaction at any one point.

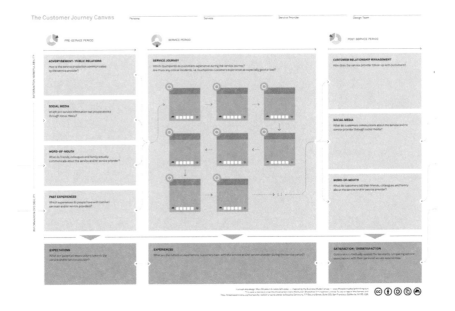

Customer journey maps are a great first step, but they are more tactical than strategic. They speak to what a company should do to get a sale, provide information, or complete a task. They do not describe the experiences that customers would like to have or what they might like from you and your company.

Wavelines solve this problem in a number of ways:

- **They use a Y-axis to show intensity** (shown in green). The intensity of any relationship experience rises and falls at different points in time. To understand how a business affects people, you need to know whether their experience is positive or negative—and how intense it is. A mildly positive reaction may not be enough to build a durable relationship. And a great one that disappears in five minutes is also not going to help. Instead, you need to evoke multiple positive experiences over time.

- **Waveline diagrams focus on the overall relationship** (shown in the light gray area). A waveline diagram outlines the effect an interaction is having and should have on a customer's state of mind. A customer journey map for a restaurant may specify that a person entering a restaurant is hungry. It charts the delivery of food, but rarely the impact on the person's well-being. The waveline diagram tells us that in an ideal interaction, the customer should leave immensely happy, thanks to a surprisingly good meal and a wonderful interaction with the wait staff.

- **Outcome matters.** Plenty of companies can make a pen that functions well. Only a few have learned to design a pen in such a way that it validates a person's sense of self every time it's used. If you want to build premium value for a brand, helping customers experience something special is the real goal. Making something that works is table stakes.

- **Wavelines make opportunities for innovation visible** (shown in yellow). If you simply compare a customer's desired waveline with the current waveline, you can find plenty of places for improvement. If a touchpoint is disappointing, that shows an area of concern (and opportunity). If it declines with no interaction, you may need to innovate a new touchpoint to keep the relationship going.

- **Wavelines map the overall experience customers have and not only the relationship with a single company** (shown in purple). United States car manufacturers are routinely caught off guard when a large jump of gas prices changes buyer priorities that make their offerings more or less attractive. The price of oil (and therefore gasoline) is something outside the car manufacturer's control, but this is a factor they must take into account as a possibility if they want to maintain a relationship through these changes.

- **Companies must be prepared to deal in real time with changes in customers' lives** (shown in red). Customers' lives are rich and complicated, and there are many changes that affect a company's relationship with their customers that come out of nowhere and create havoc. For example, when the events of September 11, 2001, occurred, people worldwide were overwhelmed by the nature and impact of these terrorist events. The reaction was so profound that it significantly changed people's wavelines, and this had an effect on customer relationships that

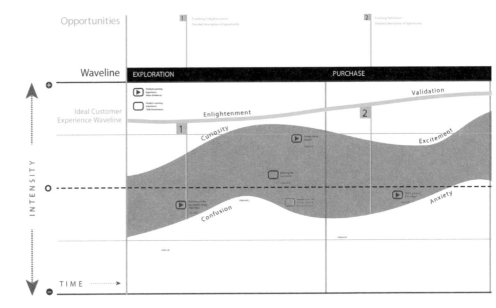

couldn't and shouldn't be ignored. For example, movie studios reacted to these sharply changed wavelines by delaying any movies they thought would be too violent or would reference sensitive subjects until they felt audiences would be more receptive to these perennial storylines. Had they not reacted in this way, their films would likely have been less successful at the box office, and they could have irreparably damaged their relationships with their viewers.

Waveline diagrams can help you develop good relationships deliberately and systematically. They can become part of your conscious strategy rather than a rare or happy accident. The next few sections look at the details of a waveline.

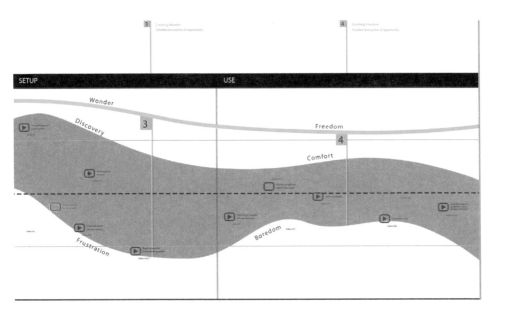

The Timeline

Every waveline diagram is based on a timeline that charts a customer's experiences over time. To understand it better, start with a waveline diagram for a mugging.

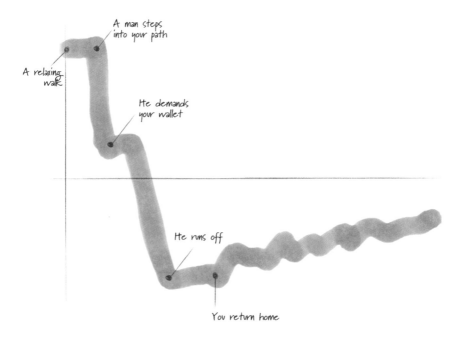

As you can see, the mugging timeline begins while you are taking your nightly walk. This is a time of relaxation and only a little intensity, normally. Then, suddenly, a man steps out from behind a tree and points a gun in your face. The waveline on the diagram drops dramatically into the negative, as you instantly shift from tranquility to panic. Muggings are, after all, extremely intense experiences. They stick with you.

Next, a demand is made. You're tense and afraid. You hand over your wallet, and your mugger then slinks away, leaving you quite relieved. You walk home and very slowly calm down. You call the police, and they come to your home quickly (gun crimes take priority). They're thorough, professional, and reassuring. You don't know if they'll ever find the guy or recover your wallet, but you do feel much better after they leave. Eventually, with the assistance of a few bourbons, you are able to relax and go to sleep.

From this, we can establish a few rules.

- **The diagram usually begins before any interaction has taken place.** Typically, a customer journey map starts at the first touch-point where a person encounters a business. The waveline has to start earlier, because you want to know the customer's state of mind prior to any interaction. And it's easy to see why—remember the Porsche ad from the previous chapter.

  Imagine you decide to buy a home entertainment system. Your emotional and experiential journey begins long before you even start researching your options on the web. It probably began when you still liked the old one you want to replace, and then a series of events happened that made you find it was less valuable.

  Next, you start looking. Given that home entertainment products inhabit a crowded and bewildering space at the moment, you will very likely be overwhelmed by your options. Your experience at that point is probably one in which you don't feel confident in making a choice about such an expensive product. As a result, a company looking to develop a relationship would probably consider how to affect that state of mind first, even though it had developed before the company had any interaction with a customer.

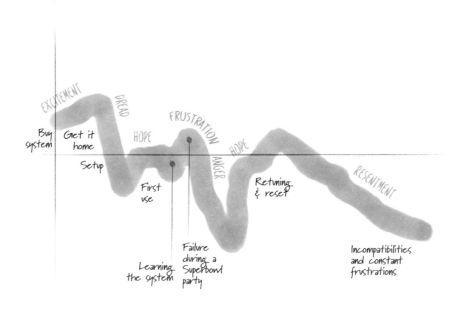

- **It depicts ongoing use. After you purchase a system, the experience isn't over.** Very often, companies focus only on driving sales. This is reasonable, but you can be amazingly good at driving sales for a product or service that disappoints time and again. Driving sales of terrible experiences won't create a relationship with customers who will come back for more. Instead, you'll drive them right into the arms of your competitors. You should not merely be driving sales but also building relationships that will lead to more reliable sales in the future.

- **It can last a lifetime.** The waveline diagram often takes much longer than a series of interactions. A coffee shop chain like Starbucks is not trying to get a customer in the door one time. The plan is for her to come in every day—even several times a day—for the rest of her life. In a good relationship, a brand or business typically stays in touch with customers either by releasing new products or features, or communicating in some way. If you're always out of sight, you'll soon be out of mind.

The Right Timeline

Given this, you might wonder if you have to plot your relationship forever. Not really. While relationships can be infinite, you have to be practical. Your time frame should be limited by the goals of your innovation effort. For example, if Starbucks wants to focus on improving its new customer acquisition efforts, it might create a waveline that takes a new customer from her first interaction up to the point she becomes a regular customer. If it wants to improve the ongoing customer experience, it would take perhaps a year-long snapshot of an existing customer's experiences. It's important to remember that the waveline diagram is just a tool. You still need to rely on your own judgment and data to determine the time frame that matters to you. That may be as short as an hour or as long as a decade.

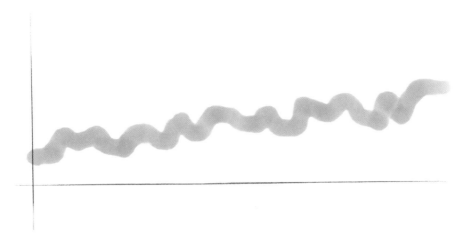

DANIEL SIEGEL ON "STATES OF MIND"

There is a real psychological underpinning for the idea that experiences cause a change in people's minds. A noted expert on the subject, Dr. Daniel Siegel, the executive director of UCLA's Mindsight Institute, describes this authoritatively:

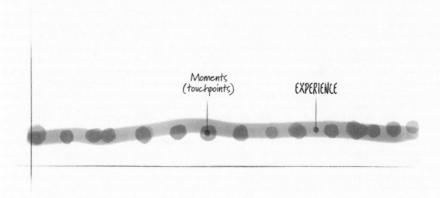

Moments
(touchpoints)

EXPERIENCE

The old paradigm of delivering products and services rests on a familiar but incomplete view of time. It views experiences in time like a string of pearls: discrete moments that are held in sequence by a thin thread that does not enhance the experiences but merely keeps one event following the next. The pearls may occasionally touch but they only superficially interact with each other.

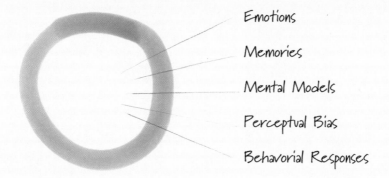

Emotions

Memories

Mental Models

Perceptual Bias

Behavorial Responses

The new paradigm is more like a tide with ebb and flow, amplitude, frequency, and other characteristics that describe the waveline of evolving states of mind over the much-longer duration of an experience. Wavelines don't occur in isolation. Physics shows how synchronized waves combine their energy. And, conversely, if completely out of sync, they cancel each other.

The mind is always seeking order and significance as a relationship evolves. You can leverage these opportunities to engage and influence relationships when you understand the systems of arousal, formation, and recall of memory. This allows you to create fluid, valuable, and more cohesive experiences at the touchpoints and in the spaces between them (along the waveline).

New paradigm developers need to make a deliberate choice: Do I develop synchronistically with an understanding of my customer's expectations over time, or choose to ignore these and focus only on my discrete deliverables? The choice must be intentional because the preparation, research, and goals will be different.[1]

---

1. Siegel, Daniel. *The Developing Mind: How Relationships and the Brain Interact to Shape Who We Are*, 2nd ed. New York: Guilford Press, 2012, p. 221.

Phases of Interaction

The second part of the waveline diagram indicates the phases of inter-action. These phases, while not always present on a waveline, generally just denote broad sweeps of time as the relationship evolves. Often, these phases will have to do with a movement from "discovery" of a possible way to meet needs, to the final running down of a product as it becomes less useful and a new phase of discovery is about to begin. Typically, these run across the top and depict overall states of mind.

A few years ago, a major health, nutrition, and weight-loss brand came to Steve's firm looking for advice. The company had created a 90-day wellness program and built an app to support it. The overall program proved popular, but the app less so. Users started using it a lot but soon stopped. The company wanted to know why and how it could improve the app.

Steve and his team dove into research and interviews. In talking with customers, they learned that their needs and desires on the third day of a diet were very different from those on the 30th. And they were different again on the 60th. Early on, people wanted the app to moti-vate them to get off the couch. Later, motivation wasn't the problem at all. By day 30 or so, they were used to working out and watching what they ate. At that point, they wanted to be reminded of their achieve-ment and urged to push themselves harder. They also wanted to brag to their friends about their progress. But the app didn't account for this. It was the same on day 1 as on day 55. Not surprisingly, most people stopped using it.

Scansion created a waveline diagram to show what was happening. In doing so, the team divided the timeline into three distinct phases based on the customers' evolving state of mind: beginning, ongoing use, and

ELEMENTS OF STATE OF MIND

There are five primary elements that, combined, define our state of mind at any time:

- Emotions (our present emotional state)
- Memories (our past experiences)
- Mental models (how we frame the world around us and how it works)
- Perceptual biases (how we, specifically, perceive stimuli in our experience)
- Behavioral responses (how we, specifically, respond to stimuli)

Each of these represents a spectrum, from global to group to individual. For example, most memories are pretty specific to personal experiences. However, you share some memories with others (things you've experienced in a group) and a few with a lot of people (such as big world events). You can't really know if any person was attacked by a dog when they were four years old (and, therefore, might have a fear of dogs), but for most people in the United States (and, to some extent, elsewhere), you share memories of the events of September 11, 2001. Unless you're developing only solutions for an individual (such as your best friend) or a small group you know well (such as those in your office), you can't incorporate individual memories.

Likewise, the other elements have some broad, shared aspects (general emotional triggers, perception generalities, general behavioral responses, and so on) and very specific group and individual ones (color blindness and hearing difficulties, intense fear at a dog barking, and so on). It's up to you as a developer to determine what you really know about the people you're developing for (where they fall across these spectra) and design accordingly and knowingly.

accomplishment. They presented it to the company's managers, who immediately saw where their opportunity lay. They hadn't considered different phases of use, but once they did, they could quickly see how they could improve the experience of their customers over time by building different experiences for each phase. Today, the app is an essential part of the company's program, and it has plenty of different motivators and rewards, including social functions that encourage people to share their success.

Just as relationships with people go through phases, so do relationships with customers. A customer's state of mind is not the same when she is shopping for your products as when she begins using them. And it's certainly different four months after that. Any good waveline diagram has to account for the changes, and it does so by adding phases of interaction.

The Intensity Axis

A central difference between a waveline and almost any other conventional touchpoint tool is two axes. The horizontal axis, naturally, is the timeline. The vertical axis shows the intensity of experience. This is an extremely important concept, because many products are perfectly functional these days. Toasters toast, and watches tell the time. Only a few make you feel like your life is worth living.

The intensity can be positive or negative. Sometimes you can try to create an intense positive experience, but it's equally valuable to relieve an intensely negative experience. In the beginning of this chapter, you saw how a mugging can greatly alter your mood. You are left panicked and fearful. Interestingly enough, some companies are aware of this and take steps to make you feel better after being robbed. And it might surprise you to find out who they are: credit card companies.

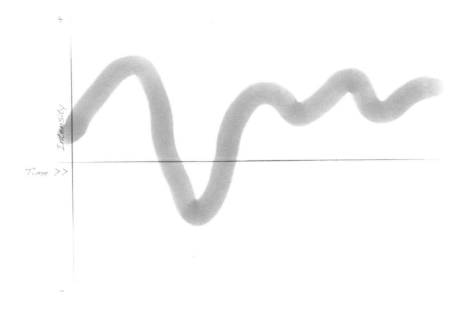

The best credit card companies know that one of your biggest fears after a mugging is that someone will run up your credit card, and you're very likely to call them while you're still shaken and upset. That's why they train their fraud and loss prevention specialists in how to soothe distressed customers. They calmly talk you through what's happened and listen to your concerns. If there are charges to your card, the credit card companies are on the hook for most of them, but there is usually a $50 deductible that you theoretically have to pay. Of course, they can waive this and often do. They can even provide you with additional information and resources to help you through the crisis. If they've done their job properly, you get off the phone relieved and thankful.

Managing the intensity axis is an important element of building a relationship. You want to continually move it up by providing experiences that are meaningful, ones that make peoples' lives better.

Wavelines

While you can, with a little practice, develop wavelines that can be used to strategize any number of situations, we've identified three primary types here: desired, expected, and current. We'll walk you through these types so that you can understand how to use them to guide an innovation process.

To understand wavelines, imagine you're the proud parent of a three-year-old boy, who is equal parts adorable and trying. While he's often fun, a slight change in his routine or simply not getting what he wants can trigger a full-blown, 15-minute screaming fit. He is also an extremely picky eater and would prefer to starve rather than try anything new. Going anywhere with him can be a nightmare.

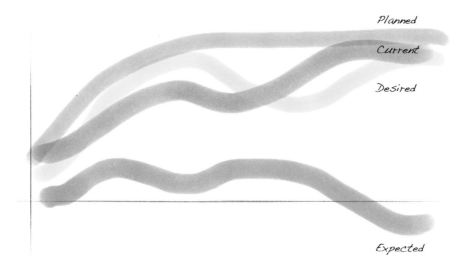

Nonetheless, you and your spouse have long wanted to take a trip to Spain. You both love the food and art, and you don't want him to dictate your experience. From a waveline standpoint, if you decide to go, there isn't just one vacation experience to keep in mind, but three: the desired, current, and expected.[2] Take a look at them and see how they work.

Desired Experience

In this experience, you imagine yourself taking a leisurely stroll through the Prado, in wonder at the insight you find in the art, while your toddler holds your hand peacefully and shows an unusual interest in the El Grecos. You're amazed that you're finally seeing the pictures from your college Art 101 class live and revel in the fact that you've gotten to Spain. After the museum, you and your spouse sip Rioja in a tapas bar. While you do this, your child is enthralled in the book you bought him at the museum and gobbles up the braised snails and squid salad.

This waveline diagram focuses on the things that happened and the way you experienced them. You increase your sense of pleasure, accomplishment, pride in your son, and self-image at nearly every touchpoint. Overall, you rise toward a crescendo of happiness that most families dream of but know not to expect.

In business, a desired waveline depicts what your customers want (not what you want): the ideal. You might think their desires are always impossible to fulfill, but that's not necessarily the case. Many times, customers do not want much from you. They may simply want to get in and out of your door as quickly as possible, with a little respect and acknowledgment. Such situations hold a lot of potential for surprising them with an unexpectedly good experience.

---

2. You reach pro status if you acknowledge these three are for each of you (including your son). Since you and your spouse are on the same wavelength so often, you can likely get by with just the one set for both of you, but you'd be advised to take into account an entirely different set for your son.

Expected Experience

Somewhere between the desired experiences people wish they could have and the one's they're actually having are the experiences they expect. Although pinning this down isn't essential when innovating improved experiences and relationships, it can be helpful in determining what your brand promise really means for people.

The expected experience(s) they anticipate, if significantly different than what they actually want, can be a danger signal that you've either overpromised or underdelivered. A serious discrepancy, at minimum, needs to be taken into account when acting on the insights from a waveline, because any promises you make moving forward may not be taken as seriously by customers as you want.

Current Experience

Imagine that you make it to Spain, and the experience turns out to not be as perfect as you want nor as bad as you probably feared. The country actually has a lot of easy food and playgrounds for kids. You spend a significant amount of time pushing your son on a swing, and in return, you get to do adult things. This is your actual experience. It has fun moments, the occasional bout of frustration, but overall, it's not bad.

For businesses, this is typically called the *current waveline.* It's how you're doing now, how your offerings are affecting the relationship you have with a customer. And although your vacation's current and desired wavelines may not be huge, the difference between the two for businesses is typically enormous. What customers want is rarely what they're getting.

That's why in creating current wavelines over the years, we've found that businesses are often startled at what they find. Sometimes, if they're of a pessimistic mind, they're pleasantly surprised to find out things aren't as bad as they thought. For most, however, the current waveline is a huge eye-opener—and not in a good way.

Using Wavelines to Design and Plan Experiences

The most important wavelines from a designing and planning perspective are, not surprisingly, the desired and current wavelines. When you can clearly see discrepancies between what people want and what they're getting, you can then ask yourself questions about how to narrow the gap between them.

You could, if desired, construct a "planned" waveline that represents your intentions to move customers' overall experiences, presumably in the direction they want. The innovation world already has a version of this type of waveline that works very well—the journey map, discussed earlier in this chapter. These maps do a great job of presenting the options available for acting on the strategic issues and choices raised by wavelines.

Often, however, it's not necessary to construct a journey map to guide innovation activities. Wavelines are representations of broad trends and strategic choices. Consequently, we've found it's sufficient to simply look at those areas of a current/desired waveline combo and ask, "Which of these discrepancies can be most cost-effectively addressed, given the relative importance they seem to have for people?"

Areas Without Interaction (and What to Do with Them)

If you're like many of us, you buy your coffee at a local café every day. Your typical experience begins when you walk in the door and ends when you throw out your paper cup. If this were charted with a waveline diagram, you'd see that the coffee drinking experience is a positive one. However, the intensity of your interaction drops to exactly nothing until you walk in to the café the next day.

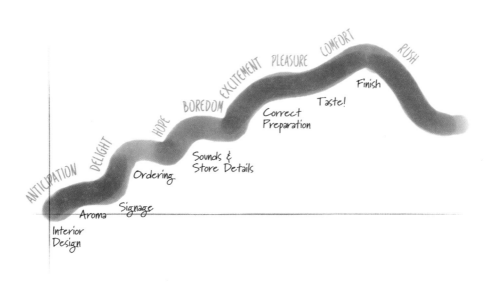

This fact is not lost on major coffee brands. Many have created apps that try to keep them in more intimate contact with their customers, beyond the part of the waveline diagram addressed by buying and drinking coffee. Some, like Starbucks, have helped turn the coffee-buying process into a seamless interaction, with welcome promotions, loyalty points, and even custom soundtracks that keep the brand in our minds more often than we otherwise would. As a result, their waveline diagrams do not drop to zero after the coffee cup is thrown out. Instead, they maintain a low-level positive interaction that lasts longer. They have a relationship with their customers.

One of the most interesting points about a waveline is that it charts the experience of a person when you're not interacting with them. It shows the dead zones as well as the moments of intense interaction.

Previously, there was not much you could do in those places; however, with social media and mobile applications, you now have every opportunity to reach out—especially when something happens that affects your clients' lives. If you do so smartly, you have a chance to build and renew your relationship more often. You may do this simply through an ad or message. Or you may respond in social media to an event not directly related to your company. In other words, you should not simply look to improve existing touchpoints, but to make new ones, where appropriate. The advantages of this are clear.

Increased Impact

Most people like it when a company fulfills their expectations. But when it exceeds them in a way or place the clients don't expect, that's even better. For instance, treating an online store as if it's an important place for customers to be pampered, as opposed to a space for incremental sales, can enhance brick-and-mortar stores' continued relevance.

Greater Connections

Today, a lot of companies drive purchases with promotions and messaging. Innovating for a more intimate, ongoing conversation allows you to foster a deeper relationship over time. One can see this sort of approach in the ads typically produced for fashion companies, in which the ad evokes the experience being promised, rather than providing "information" about functional characteristics. Often, the ads are more central to the promised experience actually being delivered than the product itself.

Greater Value

Needless to say, a loyal customer who loves your brand will pay more than average for a product. We can see this in the Apples of the world, in which the love of the brand and what it seems to stand for causes people worldwide to pay more, seemingly for comparable functionality on offer from competitors. Ultimately, people aren't paying the premium for functionality, which is generally pretty easily matched. It's the superior experience being delivered through both individual products and all the other touchpoints that make the difference.

Increased Opportunities

Even those businesses focused on designing experiences often only focus on the direct interactions (or touchpoints) in the vicinity of the experience. A waveline diagram and its spaces between touchpoints allow you to see the far greater scope for your innovation efforts.

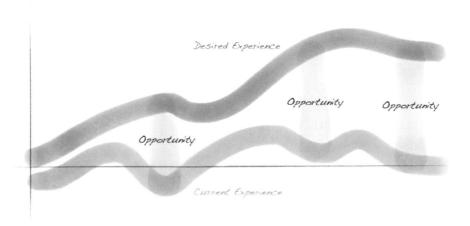

Waveline development is discussed in greater detail in Chapter 7, but here's a brief overview. Creating a waveline diagram typically involves five steps:

1. **Research the current waveline first.** You need to understand how people are actually experiencing your company through all touchpoints over time. This includes everything from products and services to advertising, PR, and events. This usually requires interviews and surveys of existing and former customers. It also demands that you collect qualitative, in addition to quantitative, data and insight.

2. **Include relevant touchpoints you don't control.** For example, if you're an appliance manufacturer, your customer's experiences

CHANGING EXPERIENCES AND WAVELINES ON THE FLY

As you saw in Chapter 2, "Defining a Business Relationship," some interactions are improvised. In other words, the company has an opportunity
to respond in a human way (often using a real human) to the concerns of
customers. These types of interactions allow you to change experiences
on the fly.

The simple truth is that you can often transform the customer's current
waveline into a better one by empowering your front-line employees
(ticket agents, customer service representatives, flight attendants, and
concierges) to make decisions themselves and go off-script when necessary, improvising with the customer in real time. You can also employ
specialists to handle unusual or difficult situations. Apple, for example, has special experts available by phone for problems that even the
geniuses at their Genius Bars can't solve.

of your brand are not solely based on you. You only make the
product and advertise it. They interact with dealers who sell your
product and the third-party service people who install it. All of
them have an impact on the customer relationship.

3. **Find out what moves your customers.** Your research should
   always uncover what's missing, what customers want, and what
   provides them with a more valuable experience. This requires
   research into their states of mind at different points in the relationship. If you are only researching product features and price
   points, you'll miss out on big opportunities to innovate.

4. **Construct a great desired waveline.** This waveline should
   tell a compelling story that is satisfying for both the company
   and the customer. Even if you're already doing a great job with
   your customer relationships, this will expose opportunities
   for improvement.

5. **Identify opportunities for innovation.** Your best opportunities for innovation, or opportunity spaces, occur at places where the current and desired waveline diverge the most. These could either be at existing touchpoints or between touchpoints. Either way, you'll easily be able to find them whenever you construct a waveline diagram.

Segmenting for Waveline Diagrams

Over time, businesses can get hung up on the idea that people's experiences can vary greatly. Some believe that this makes it impossible to chart experiences over time. A tech-savvy teenager does not interact with a smartphone the way Grandma does. A novice cook does not use an oven the way an experienced baker does. A person who buys goat's milk as a novelty has a different experience of it than a person who buys it because she's allergic to other kinds of milk.

In addition, pretty much everyone has a different experience of a brand, depending on their mood, life experience, time of day, or any number of factors. You might enjoy the morning news one day if you've had a good breakfast, and not at all the next if you've had none. Given all of this, you might be wondering how you can plan a waveline at all. In the following sections, you'll find several reasons why this is not actually a problem.

Using Wavelines to Describe a Combination of Experiences

Wavelines offer a 10,000-foot view and are typically built by researching many customers' experiences and aggregating them into separate wavelines—or two or three—where the customer segments are distinct.

Needing to Generalize

You could, for example, construct a waveline for a single event for one person, but you can't do that for an entire market. Therefore, you need to generalize and stick to the combinations of experiences that reflect a set of customers.

Diminishing Marginal Returns

Theoretically, you can create a waveline diagram for a large market or just one person. Obviously, most businesses will quickly deduce that their costs of innovation start to exceed any benefit from it if they target too many distinct wavelines.

Segmenting Customers the Right Way

The most common mistake companies make in segmenting their customers is to rely on demographics or product features. This can help you satisfy your customers functionally, but not in a truly valuable way, because anyone can fill their needs. Premium value only emerges when you understand and provide the experiences that your customers desire.

That's why you should typically segment by surveying customers about the experiences they deeply want. Look at who they really are, not merely what category they fall into. All mothers aged 22 to 30 do not want the same things. Some will be impressed and affected by certain kinds of interactions; others not so much. That's why, in addition to the usual demographic details, try to focus on a few key questions:

1. What emotional needs do they have?

2. What do they want out of interactions?

3. How do they see their identity? Who they are, and how they would like to be seen?

4. What do they desire experientially? (This is in a holistic sense, not a simple one. You want to know what they want out of life, not merely out of you.)

5. What makes life worth living for them? In this, look at the kinds of meaningful experiences they really treasure, so that you can either provide the same, or not impede it.

In other words, you segment by what *outcome* they want from their interactions with your company. And you can only do this by knowing what they want as people and then filtering that down to the kinds of items and experiences you can provide.

EYE OPENERS

In this chapter, you learned about a new tool, the waveline diagram, which is designed to help companies understand and evolve their relationships with customers strategically. You saw how the waveline contains a number of critical elements:

- A timeline that stretches across the customer's total range of experiences evoked by touchpoints.

- Phases of engagement that show the overall expectations of a customer during different phases of development of relationships with customers.

- A Y-axis that shows the intensity of the experiences a customer has or wants from us.

- Touchpoints, where customers interact with an organization.

- Experiences before, during, and after any interaction.

- A current waveline depicting the experiences and overall relationship customers have today.

- A desired waveline that shows what experiences and relationship your clients want to have.

You also learned how to deal with experiences you can't control and find the right waveline for you. However, here are some questions to get you thinking:

- How would a waveline change your approach to your customers?

- What does your current waveline look like?

- What are the reasons to develop multiple wavelines in your case?

- How likely is it that there's a certain fear within your organization to uncover the actual experiential situation your customers are facing? If so, how can you address that?

- What untapped areas exist in your interactions with customers, spaces where you're not interacting with customers and where innovation could really make a difference?

- What would your ideal customer relationships look like?

4

Finding Opportunities in Relationships

Many organizations create good experiences and foster long-term relationships, but few do so consciously, and they don't know what to do when the ground shifts beneath them. They often accomplish this *despite* the processes and metrics they use internally. If those relationships eventually go south, they don't know how to innovate to recover.

This chapter will look at a number of different types of relationships and experiences. This will give you an idea of what they look like, even when they're not consciously created. You'll also see how you can use visual tools to catch growing concerns and set the stage for conscious, deliberate innovation around relationships. Finally, you'll learn why less rigid, more free-form interactions—co-created or improvised—tend to work better over time.

Getting It Right the Wrong Way

In the last few years, a number of cooking shows have cropped up in which a famous chef challenges a much-less-celebrated cook, who is nonetheless known for one particular dish. For example, the show *Throwdown with Bobby Flay* pits the Food Network star against local celebrities known for American classics like chicken and biscuits or turkey chili. A British show, *The F Word,* more tellingly pits Gordon Ramsay, whose restaurants have won 16 Michelin stars, against British celebrities who cook simple homemade favorites.

You might think the amateurs would have no chance against world-renowned chefs, but it's quite the opposite. The more celebrated chef typically loses more often than not. It may seem ludicrous that Flay cannot defeat a relative "nobody" making a roast beef sandwich, or that Ramsay cannot defeat an amateur making a curry. However, by concentrating on one thing, and making it thousands of times, untrained cooks often leapfrog in quality over even the best chefs in the world. The problem is that the amateurs often don't often know why they do the things they do. They almost certainly can't apply the principles underlying their best dish elsewhere. If, at the last moment, they were asked to compete in soup rather than chili, they would always lose.

Something similar happens in business relationships. Very few individual businesses build relationships consciously. The Disneys, Teslas, Apples, and Cartiers of the world are rare. But together and over time, companies often hit on a formula that works reasonably well. Of course, this can be as much of a problem as it is a good thing. Complacency can set in. Too often, companies begin looking for greater efficiency instead of continuous improvement. Over time, they actually forget how to improve their relationships.

Eventually, the hammer falls, and disruption comes. They get asked to make chicken soup, and they don't know how. They don't know why what they were doing worked so well—or how to apply that knowledge to new circumstances. They simply know how to do one thing well, and when customers no longer want that one thing, they can't adapt.

A formerly great business like Borders Books or Kodak can easily get blindsided by change—and more often than not, it's because of complacency of management or fear of cannibalization, rather than not being inspired to innovate. Best Buy was long considered one of the most innovative retailers in the world, but it struggled when the Internet gobbled up much of its business. If its management had been paying attention to their customer relationships and was sensitive to why they were good and working, they'd have seen that those cozy old friendships were changing, and people were growing rapidly dissatisfied.

Kodak actually tried this strategy in 1996, in a project called Kodak Picture Network. Nathan's company at the time, **vivid** studios, worked with a team at Kodak to build the first online photo-sharing network. This would have enabled different kinds of relationships. But this team couldn't get approval within Kodak's leadership because their leaders neither understood the medium nor wanted one division within Kodak competing against others. By the time they changed their mind and started to pursue this kind of online relationship, it was way too late; they didn't stick with it and turned instead to the tried and tired business techniques of slashing margins and pushing employees to sell things customers didn't want. In this case, management should have panicked much earlier and driven themselves to reinvent and improve.

Most theories about innovation speak about having a radar for changes in the marketplace and continuously pivoting to come up with new ideas of your own. In fact, no one exactly knows which disruptions matter—except your customers. It's better to simply look at your relationships to understand why circumstances have changed, rather than try to figure out on your own which way the wind is blowing and why it changed direction.

Short-Term, Climax-Driven Experiences

Imagine a woman and her simple interaction with a company, such as her first visit to a local coffee shop. Over the course of five minutes, her anticipation slowly builds, as does the intensity. The journey begins when she feels thirsty and then finds and walks into the store, where she sees a skilled barista working the espresso machine. She smells freshly roasted beans, which increases her appetite for a cup. Her anticipation rises again when she reads the menu, finds something she wants, orders, and so on, up until the climactic moment when she takes her first sip. If it's delicious, she's thrilled.

This is a classic way to structure a sequence of experiences, and it's one that many companies should strive to emulate. In it, you create anticipation and then overdeliver on satisfaction. Of course, companies may fail to get there. The barista might not be skilled or attentive, and the menu may not have what the customer really wants. In those cases, the actual experiences don't match the desired ones, and disappointment will follow. To build a great coffee touchpoint, you need to make sure that everything works together. The menu must be comprehensive without being overwhelming. The product line should not be too complicated. The smell of roasted beans should be present but not overpowering, and so on. If you want to make the experiences exceptional, focus on providing quality, options, friendliness, and the right rhythm of interaction. Everything except the coffee and the interaction with the barista should be so easy and obvious that it drops away as part of the experience.

You can visualize this through a waveline diagram. Its timeline starts before the initial touchpoint and extends after it because the customer's experience of buying coffee begins when she first feels the need for something to drink. If it's morning, coffee might be part of a ritual. If it's afternoon, she's probably either listless or bored at work. In the evening, she's likely on a social visit. Needless to say, the smart owner and staff at a coffee shop would vary the characteristics of the store at different times of day, rotating the snacks, changing the music, and adjusting the lighting.

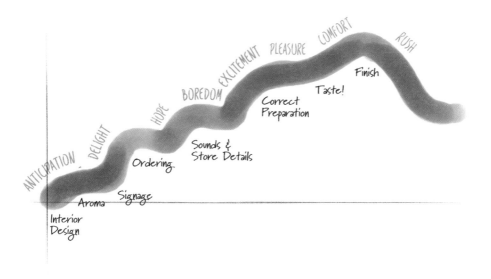

Longer-Term Relationships

Great relationships do not always look like great interactions. If you have a terrific lawnmower, your experience of it probably began as a dread of having to cut your grass. The waveline then flips to positive, thanks to the unexpected ease with which you complete the task and your happiness at having it in the rearview mirror. Your positive relationship toward the tool builds as you have great experiences over time. Eventually, you love the thing because it makes your life easier than you thought it could be.

When you visualize that kind of relationship, it looks much more like a wave that moves up and down over time. Each high point in the wave corresponds to the climax in the sequence of experiences, while the low points occur as you slowly realize the grass is getting out of hand again.

You can also look at this through the lens of the coffee shop example. Imagine your customer goes there once a week for a month. You can diagram her relationship with the shop as it grows, by looking at both her store experiences and other aspects of her interaction: memories of the way she felt physically each time she went, interactions with friends and employees there, and even advertisements related to the company and its products. All of these contribute to an evolving relationship that hopefully gets better over time.

Threats to Longer-Term Relationships

It's important to realize that a slow rise in positive feelings does not occur in every case. From a strategic standpoint, there are three threats to any good, long-term relationship: outside developments, habituation, and losing touch with customer needs and desires.

OUTSIDE DEVELOPMENTS

Many companies with formerly good relationships fall down because they fail to detect changes in their customer perceptions of their products or their category. As mentioned earlier in this chapter, Best Buy got into trouble not only because online retailers sold for less, but also because it didn't respond to how customers wanted to shop and how they wanted to be treated.

Some businesses, however, are good at shifting with changes in climate. Successful health food businesses, for example, are continually buffeted by the public's fascination with new food fads. Over the years, they have had to contend with wild lurches in public perception of salt, fats, cholesterol, carbohydrates, calories, and sugar—not to mention, the rise of "superfoods" like kale, kambutcha, quinoa, and chia seeds. In the last decade alone, they weathered a raw food movement, a rise in veganism, high-protein diets, locovorism, the Paleo diet, and numerous others. Any company in such a field needs to be sensitive to changes in customer perceptions of what *healthy* means and innovatively evolve their offerings to stay on top of them.

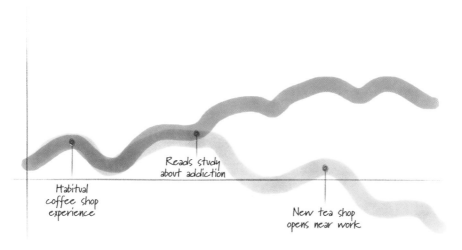

It's important to note, as is clear from this example, that the changes you have to make need not be rational or right. Many a company fails when it tries to affect a cultural shift by arguing against it. Chocolate companies, for example, recently faced a wave of sensationalist reports of child labor and harsh working conditions on cocoa farms. Those companies sit at a great distance in the supply chain from actual farms and have almost no influence on working conditions. But wisely, they have not contested the reports or protested their innocence. Instead, they have quietly instituted programs to try to reach out to farmers and find ways to improve their lives.[1] Companies must constantly stay abreast of their customers' lives to understand the effects these outside developments have and prepare to react appropriately, if necessary.

1. Inter alia, see Mars' Sustainable Cocoa Initiative: www.cocoasustainability.com.

HABITUATION

Habituation occurs in almost any situation in which the touchpoints remain the same. As mentioned previously, customers become accustomed to an experience, and it becomes less intense and meaningful to them—just as a song, played 100 times, will go from being emotionally inspiring to completely uninteresting. Businesses that are able to renew the excitement from time to time do much better in developing strong relationships with their customers.

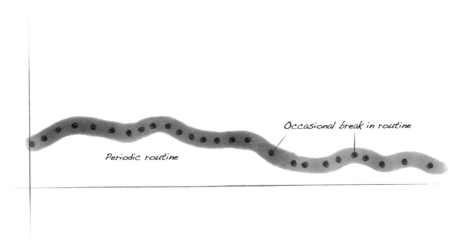

Periodic routine

Occasional break in routine

Some industries are good at disrupting the cycle of habituation. The television industry, for example, has developed many ways to keep tension and interest for viewers of recurring episodes. For example, the cliff-hanger, flashback, and prequel are designed to surprise, shock, and raise intensity in the narrative, just when interest might be waning or to last between episodes or seasons.

LOSING TOUCH WITH CUSTOMER NEEDS AND DESIRES

Success is often its own undoing. After a company successfully understands its customers and what they need, methods and processes are introduced to keep delivering on those promises. People in operations do their best to standardize, speed up, and smooth down processes so that everyone's lives in the supply chain are easier and more predictable. Naturally, this helps increase profitability in the short term.

The challenge is that companies that do this often miss when their successful formula starts to waver, wane, or the factors that drive customer decisions shift. That might happen due to outside influences, competitors, or market forces. But it can also happen because customers change their minds or goals. If your eye is only on features, or technology, or the market, you miss these changes because relationships aren't about any of those.

Relationships are a continuous process, requiring continuous contact and understanding. You can find forces of stability in them (meanings, priorities, and identities come to mind), but how you touch on those things can change rapidly. A famous ad for Yuban coffee once touched on a wife's surprise when her husband decided to have an extra cup of coffee at a party. "Jim never has a second cup at home," she thinks, disappointed. Today, the message seems dated and sexist, and the brand wisely stays away from it. It still cares about portraying itself as delivering a satisfying cup of coffee—but not in that way. Instead, today it's the only national brand offering a full line of Rainforest Alliance Certified coffee.

Lifetime Relationships

Now, imagine that the coffee shop customer eventually visits the store, on and off, for her entire adult life. In this case, the waveline depicts her evolving relationship. Every few months or so, her positive intensity spikes upward as the shop provides new things she wants to try. It might be the peppermint latte at Christmas, upgraded furniture, faster Wi-Fi, or just a comfy sofa where she can meet her friends and colleagues. This constant renewal of interest, not to mention the good coffee, keeps her satisfied and coming back for more.

For a child, a lifetime relationship with Disney and Disneyland would develop quite differently. Naturally, the intensity of the experience will fade for her—after all, Disney is nice, but eventually Mickey Mouse loses his ability to fascinate. Yet, she still will retain somewhere a positive feeling toward the brand. It's up to Disney to reactivate that in her when she or other members of her family have children.

The important thing is that as humans, we strive for relationships that last as long as is practical and possible.

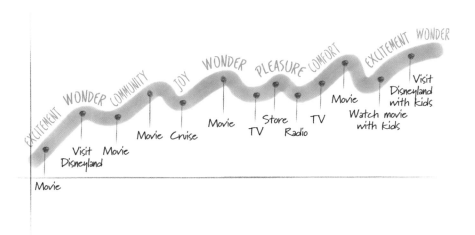

Touchpoint Categories

The next few pages look at the challenges and opportunities for innovation in a number of broad categories and industries to understand how waveline diagrams can work and look. These include:

- Products
- Services
- Events
- Environments
- Gaming
- Hospitality

The first four cover virtually any type of offering-oriented touch-point (as opposed to advertising or PR)—certainly the vast majority. Almost everything your organization offers will fall into these four categories. (See Chapter 2, "Defining a Business Relationship," for more discussion of touchpoints and their roles in evoking experiences that build relationships.)

It's worth mentioning that within any category there are likely to be a few standard wavelines that are commonly used because they represent expectations within customers. For television shows, there are common formats of romantic comedies, dramas, situation comedies, and so on that have well-worn patterns. The wavelines for these and even products may look identical with competitors' offerings before any innovation process. That's exactly the opportunity, however. By innovating the relationship, possibilities to step outside of formulas and develop better connections with customers exist that transcend expectations.

To show how relationships play out in specific industries, hospitality and gaming can be used as examples because they offer good models for how different experiences can be when customers enter these worlds. Customers interact with the hospitality industry, for example—hotels, spas, restaurants, and even travel—with profoundly different individual goals and needs. When gaming, players have much different expectations from those they have when they're in the real world. By exploring these relationships, you can understand the flexibility and strength of a waveline diagram for describing experiences and relationships.

Products

At first glance, physical products like your refrigerator don't appear to evolve, and you can't imagine them developing a relationship with you. However, your experience with products changes over time as you use and understand them from different perspectives. They get more familiar. They become more useful. Sometimes, they reveal physical and functional qualities that you didn't originally notice, such as the built-in first-aid kit sitting in the passenger compartment of some models of Mercedes-Benz and Saab or the emergency flashers built in to the doors of some cars that you would never notice until you're pulled over on the side of the road at night. To create and support a relationship built on what people want, you need to understand how this happens.

Overall, products change in three major ways over time: qualities, use, and aging.

QUALITIES

You may think a wooden chair is simply a chair, and there is nothing more to it. You buy it, you sit on it, and it's either comfortable or not. But, in fact, chairs are among the most difficult of all products to design because your use of and experience with one differ greatly over time. A straight-backed chair looks and feels one way at a dinner table. It appears different if you look at it from another angle or sit in it in a different position. Your experience with the chair can even change if you gain some weight. If you move the chair to a different place, you can dramatically change the way it is perceived and its impact on you. (Think of how strange your kitchen chairs would look in a living room, or how uncomfortable a bar stool is without a bar on which to rest your elbows.) If a chair manufacturer wants customers to love its chair, the company must pay attention to the vast range of possible uses and locations.

Products all have qualities that are revealed over time. A cheap knife cuts perfectly well at first, but, in short order, the blade gets dull and can no longer be sharpened. The waveline diagram that describes the use of that knife would start out fairly well and then slowly turn negative. The customer relationship would end as well—especially if the knife couldn't be sharpened.

DIFFERENT USES

A more complex product, like a mobile phone, does not change much physically over time. It always has the same processor, buttons, memory, and screen. But the sheer number of uses it has enables it to evolve over time in significant ways. Operating system upgrades give it different capabilities every year or so, and that changes the way you interact with and experience it. New apps will come along, and others will be upgraded. A phone company that wants to design and maintain a relationship with a customer should ensure that a product of this kind reveals its qualities in a pleasing way over time. Many have noted that the vast feature set of the iPhone makes owning one such a pleasure, because users continually learn things that they didn't know the phone could do. In addition, the features are often upgraded and expanded with new versions of the operating system. In this way, the touchpoint can evolve and improve even after its purchase. Still, to others, it's daunting and scary to learn everything they need to in order to use one effectively.

AGING

Here's the bad news. All products age, and usually aging is bad. There are some exceptions, of course: a fine wine is best aged (though not too much). Some people prefer jeans when they have a broken-in look. Today, because the mass-produced, mid-century modern furniture is so popular, original examples in good condition sell for vast multiples of what they originally did. Most of the time, however, aging degrades a product. Mid-century furniture's rise to treasured antique status followed a long period in which such products were seen as cheap, lowbrow, and overly simplified trash.

Aging affects products primarily in three ways:

- **Deterioration.** Things get beat up and fall apart. They lose their functionality and structure. They get scratched, dented, and wear out. Eventually, they look old and many times stop acting like they should.

- **Taste.** You may have liked bell bottoms in the 1970s, hated them in the 80s, and rediscovered them in the late 90s. People always look for new stimulation, and they habituate quickly to materials and colors. Today, foodies have fallen in love with New Nordic cuisine and are feasting on pickled lichens and oak bark ice cream. Ten years ago, no one in their right mind would have eaten such things, and it's very likely they won't in ten more years either. Tastes always change.

- **Replacement competition.** Unless you've broken your old smartphone or dropped it in the ocean, it probably functions exactly as it did when you bought it. Still, newer phones have come out with better functionality, bigger screens, and a cooler look. New things make most people feel like the old thing no longer meets specific needs, so it's off to purchase new things.

Products change, and when they do, relationships to them also change. Or they stay the same, but the consumers change. That's why a product relationship diagram (shopping for and purchasing a new chair) often looks like that shown in the following figure.

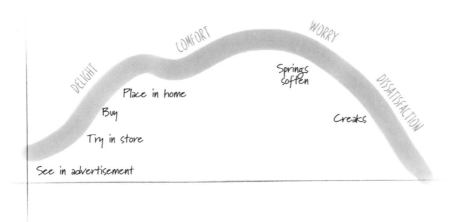

CLASSIC PRODUCTS

Of course, some products don't degrade over time. In a few categories, you can create something that outlasts trends and becomes a classic that owners do not part with. KitchenAid stand mixers offer a good example; however, you're usually not going to be that lucky. With digital technologies, disruptive change, and new contexts, you can expect most products to become obsolete or unwanted—and you need to plan for that.

Services

Products are objects, and therefore feel more tangible than most services. However, both deliver tangible and intangible benefits. Because services often require more interaction between a customer and a system, they are a lot easier to understand in relationship terms and often much easier to manage. For example, imagine that you need to prepare a will. You ask around, and a friend recommends a lawyer. You call her, and from the moment you walk into her office she's attentive to all of your needs. She knows this is a stressful time for you, as no one likes to make provisions for their own death. Nonetheless, she quickly acknowledges your feelings and puts you at ease about everything: costs, making sure it's done right, and making sure you understand the process. You give her all of your information, and a few days later, she invites you back to talk through the will's provisions.

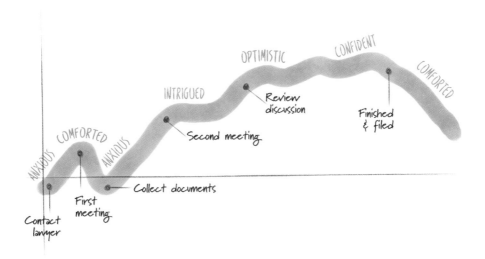

What makes this sequence of experiences and emotions so successful? First, your attorney responded to what she knew about people making wills: they're usually uncomfortable. She acknowledged that your fears were reasonable and made you feel better about them. She had a warm sense of humor. And she made a scary topic understandable and accessible to you.

Second, she determined the pace, rhythm, and intensity of the experiences according to how fast she thought you could process new information. She didn't put you on her most efficient timetable. For her, it would be best for her to simply knock out the will as quickly as possible. But instead she got on your timeline.

She also probably charged you more than you needed to pay. Wills are not usually complicated—in fact, you can make one online. You were not paying for her skill. Instead, she charged a premium because she knew how to handle the relationship in the right way. You would likely get the same will from another lawyer, but a much different experience, with a lower level of comfort and trust. And possibly a lower price.

In fact, the value found in services does not usually come from the thing a service does. Almost all dentists can fill cavities—only some can make sitting in their chairs a pleasant or reassuring experience. Many services aren't designed to give employees much leeway in shaping the customer's experience and, hence, the relationship. In automated phone systems, for example, you typically have only a certain number of possible interactions. Not surprisingly, they're usually considered annoying.

When visualizing services, most waveline diagrams—especially for customer service—are similar to those for music or movies. They rise in intensity, releasing at a pivotal point, because the moment when the answer is given or the document is presented is when the customer reaches the climax of the narrative. The rest is just pleasantries (thank you and have a nice day).

The same attributes that affect the aging of products (deterioration, taste, and replacement competition) can apply to services with one exception: deterioration doesn't happen in a physical sense. Services have an easier time evolving over time because there's no physical object that needs to be upgraded.

Events

Most companies host events—whether it's a simple Christmas party, a gigantic industry gathering like Oracle's OpenWorld, or even one of Apple's carefully scripted announcements. Some are even in the event business, like concert managers or theaters.

You might think that the critical difference between an event and a product or service is that it is shorter in duration. This isn't necessarily so. Events actually linger for a long time. A Christmas party might be considered successful if an employee receives a gift that helps him in his work. It is unsuccessful if the boss gets drunk and starts telling everyone he really thinks they're idiots.

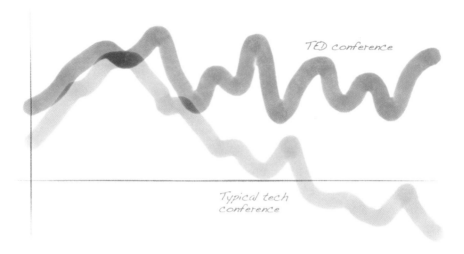

One real-world example is a waveline of a TED Conference, which generally stays stimulating and enlightening for the entire event versus a typical tech conference, which frequently becomes progressively less compelling, experientially, as it goes on. With TED, we remember multiple speakers, who can have a powerful impact for us to the very end and beyond.

In other words, good events live long after in your memory. The residual feelings they create can be powerful, even after the memories start to fade.

Many corporate event planners assume that with online and social technologies, the need for events is fading. Some believe they're "not worth it," referring to the expense of physically gathering people. This seems short-sighted, however. Whereas a lot can be accomplished today via the Internet, cell phones, and more that used to be required by face-to-face interaction, there is still a lot of value in being physically present. Some relationships can only be developed in person—especially if the relationship is crucial.

Environments

Environments can be physical spaces, such as forests, parks, galleries, casinos, lobbies, offices, and shopping malls; or they can be virtual, such as websites, applications, or simulations. Needless to say, you should take the evolution of experience into account when creating or innovating for either kind of environment. Take for instance, a typical casino waveline. While often designed to keep us distracted from leaving by blinking lights and compelling sounds, the actual waveline, by taking the entire evolving experience into account, suggests that the relationship being built isn't all that satisfying.

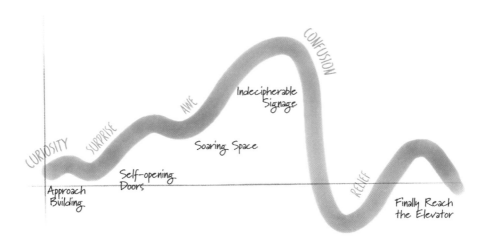

Next, identify what you expect people to do in these spaces. As you learned with our curatorial example in Chapter 2, people move in predictable ways, and you should anticipate their movement and shape your offerings accordingly.

Finally, consider how the space is used over time. Imagine, for example, you're walking up the steps of the Lincoln Memorial. The building is designed in such a way that it slowly reveals the statue of Abraham Lincoln in dramatic fashion. You first see Lincoln's head peeking over the stairs. Then slowly he comes into view, looming over his visitors as you venture closer. When you get inside, you can read the inscriptions (his second inaugural and Gettysburg addresses among them). The entire process has been carefully considered and staged to produce a certain kind of experience with a distinct pace. It's practically cinematic.

Whereas the Lincoln Memorial offers a narrative experience, you can also think of time in a more practical way. Most corporate lobbies, for example, are environments designed for a grand entrance. They are made to impress a new customer, prospect, or investor when they first encounter the company. The problem is that when creating a lobby, a designer should also look at how it functions on a daily basis. Lobbies often waste space that could be used for other tasks and items. They're also loud due to many hard surfaces and high ceilings, and it's annoying to sign in at a dramatically tall receptionist's desk. Add a security screening area, and it quickly becomes not only a hassle but an unwelcoming place. Although the first impressions are dramatic, they can be annoying on a day-to-day basis.

Gaming

Games offer a very different perspective on relationships. Unlike coffee shops, they don't drive to a climax. Rather, they are designed to maintain a constant level of tension and intensity for long periods, or they allow the intensity to drop and stay low for a while as well. This is especially true of massively, multiplayer, nonlinear games like *World of Warcraft*.

Role-playing games like these can go on for hours. A good game creator understands the rhythm of expectations she thinks will work, as well as the different levels of intensity that customers want at different times.

Modern games also usually give the player a lot of freedom in how the experience develops—at least as much as their skill level allows. Using a relationship diagram can ensure that this intensity is expected and that new players are on board in a positive way, while existing players are still challenged and rewarded enough to keep playing.

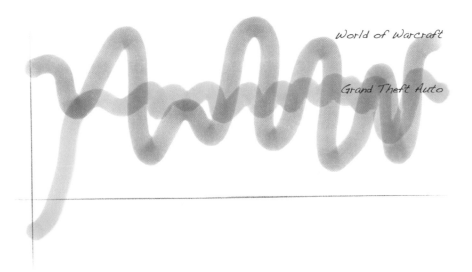

World of Warcraft

Grand Theft Auto

Hospitality

The hospitality industry offers another example of where our expectations and desires are quite different from ordinary products and services. However, at the end of the day, the typical hospitality waveline looks a lot like Toch's classic one shown in Chapter 3, "Visualizing Relationships."

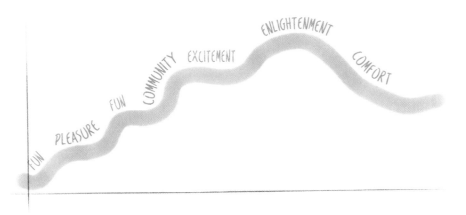

FUN PLEASURE FUN COMMUNITY EXCITEMENT ENLIGHTENMENT COMFORT

Imagine you're visiting an all-inclusive Caribbean resort for four days with your spouse and two kids You're looking forward to the beaches, water skiing, swimming, fishing, yoga classes, and many other things, including a swim-up bar. Of course, your experiential waveline begins well before you arrive, because you plan and anticipate what you're going to do when you get there.

When you arrive, you encounter the palm trees, architecture, music, and broader atmospherics that all say "tropical paradise." You and your family have an immediate endorphin rush. It's starting off great.

After check-in by a warm and courteous staff person, you're escorted to your suite, again with impeccable service. The rooms reinforce the sense of well-being and pleasure you're already experiencing, particularly that great view of both the pool and the sea. The staff offer to unpack for you all if you like, but your kids like to do it themselves (go figure!), so you thank your room attendants and let the kids take care of it.

What follows is four days of enjoyment, punctuated by the occasional annoyance (the fishing boat is just a bit "off" in some way you can't put your finger on, for instance), and the kids require a bit more forceful discipline by the pool than should be necessary at their ages. But over-all, everything's gone well.

The afternoon of the third day, you go on a tour of the local fishing vil-lage. You didn't expect much from this—just a way to spend the time, really—but you were moved by the sheer beauty of the life all around you. Turns out the locals lead quietly amazing lives, and although you hadn't expected or even wanted a culturally enriching trip, that's what you got. That tour turned out to be the high point of the entire vaca-tion, surprisingly enhancing the overall enjoyment. As you fly home, you and your family talk about how great this trip was, and you think to yourself about how it seems like, if you're away four days, usually the high point of the trip is three days in. But if you're gone ten days, the high point is on the eighth day. Strange.

The high point of a trip, quite frequently, happens when you're primed for it, which usually is when you have a sense, if unconscious, that you're around 70 percent of the way into it. Some might argue that you're anticipating the climax of the narrative of your trips, and so you tend to choose activities (or mindsets) that get you to that high point. It certainly isn't guaranteed, but it does seem to be the case. Hence, the waveline.

EYE OPENERS

This chapter looked at a range of different kinds of relationships and some of the opportunities where companies can improve them. You saw that in almost any category there are expectations you must meet and radical ideas that you might use to innovate for the relationship and provide more value.

Some food for thought:

- To what extent is your company consciously thinking of relationships over time?

- In what ways are you allowing your customers to have a great experience, or managing their experiences?

- List all of the experiences you design and deliver. (Hint: every touchpoint for which your organization is responsible evokes an experience.)

- How does your product or service differ from the waveline diagrams shown in this chapter?

5

Becoming by Doing

E ngaging in an innovation process specifically to deepen relationships is, generally speaking, a process that engages many parts of an organization and often needs them to change in both big and small ways. This is not merely in terms of developing new products and services, but also for how you deliver them. That's why it's important to look at "relationship innovation" through a holistic lens. It's not a simple or easy process, and the place to start is from the ground up to ensure not only that you change in the right way for your customers, but also that the organization is ready to change as well.

These changes can best happen through a process called *becoming by doing.* It involves not merely coming up with great ideas for new products and services, but also laying the groundwork to transform organizations as well.

The Innovation Conundrum

Over the last century, a number of books and articles have been written about innovation: what it is, how to do it, and why one approach works better than another. It might seem a little presumptuous to try to add anything to the conversation, but relationships are different, and innovation for them requires a new approach.

Start with a few general observations about innovation itself. In essence, all innovation processes are about growing a company and building value. But as you innovate successfully and your organization grows larger, most companies find it increasingly difficult to come up with and incorporate new ideas. They find it hard to consistently predict what customers are going to do and like. More importantly, after companies reach a certain size, they begin to focus an increasing proportion of their efforts on efficiency and standardizing processes. After you've built a great business, you need to maintain that business. You want to protect it and maximize its potential. In other words, you have an *innovation conundrum*. It states that a track record of successful innovation usually leads to a situation that deters further innovation.

If you're familiar with the archetypal Hero's Journey, you may find that the design phase, indeed the entire process of becoming by doing, could play out as a quest within your organization to accomplish what is deemed impossible and come back with a new treasure: an innovative solution. Of course, like any hero's journey, you will be tested along the way, with trials and obstacles posed by both peers and policies. Legacy ideas about "how things are" and "how we do things here" need to be overcome—they always do. Even just a little time spent devising a strategy for how to engage others within the design process—and when—can pay off with a smoother experience.

THE HERO'S JOURNEY

In 1949, author and mythologist, Joseph Campbell, introduced the concept of the *hero's journey* as a common structure for stories throughout many cultures. His book, *The Hero with a Thousand Faces,* told of the similar narrative structures of heroes, from Buddha, Moses, and Jesus to those in popular media, like Disney films or *Star Wars.* That these narratives have similarities is a testament to the power of a successful waveline. The streamlined 12 steps from the "known" world into the "unknown" and back again recur endlessly in many cultures because they build drama, relieve tension, build again, and then climax in a pleasing, adventurous way.

Campbell's 12 stages include:

1. The Ordinary World
2. The Call to Adventure
3. Refusal of the Call
4. Meeting with the Mentor
5. Crossing the Threshold (to the unknown world)
6. Tests, Allies, and Enemies
7. Approach the Innermost Cave
8. The Ordeal
9. The Reward
10. The Road Back
11. The Resurrection
12. Return with the Elixir

These stages are, of course, generalized, but we can find thousands of examples of variations on this structure. In addition, it's not unlike contemporary, real experiences, such as innovating within a large organization. Innovators face many challenges trying to make change in the world (and in their organizations), which aren't always different than the challenges, trials, allies, and enemies faced by the heroes in these stories.

Cultural Antibodies

Darrel Rhea, an innovation consultant and former CEO of Added Value Cheskin, has written extensively about the challenges of innovating, particularly in companies that are financially successful. He points out that such companies often have what he calls "cultural antibodies" to innovation. These are engrained practices or attitudes in an organization that oppose anything that interferes with or complicates day-to-day operations. Cultural antibodies are not a consciously created set of attitudes. If asked directly, most people in the organization would say they are open to innovation. They do not want to kill great ideas. But it happens nonetheless. When people have a good business to protect, they often see new initiatives as distractions to ongoing success.

Jeanne Leidtka, who teaches at the University of Virginia's Darden School of Business, talks about this in her books as well. In *The Catalysts,* she and her co-authors write about how the very actions and orientations that make innovation successful are often offenses that can get an innovator fired in most larger companies. This is because innovation isn't efficient nor a sure thing, and most managers aren't willing to suspend their disbelief for the required length of time.

The Incubator Problem

A common solution to the problem of cultural antibodies is to create an incubator, a space for innovation outside of the existing structures in a company. Xerox PARC is probably the most famous of these, mainly because of the many successful companies it spawned, such as Adobe and Sun, generally with little benefit to Xerox. With modern innovation labs, the idea is to segregate an innovation project for a period of time. That gives the budding idea the protection it needs to grow safely until it's ready to be introduced into company processes or the market at large. Companies that grow successfully by acquisition do much the same thing. They buy another business only when it's mature enough to fend for itself in the larger organization.

Of course, both of these approaches to solving resistance to new ideas have spotty track records. Few larger companies successfully innovate by incubator. And acquisitions are difficult. For every smart and successful one, we find a dozen (or more) failures. In both cases, this happens because of the cultural mismatch between what it takes to innovate and what it takes to implement. When the clash comes, the cultural antibodies rise up and rule.

Cultural Toxicity

Some have argued that large corporate culture is usually toxic to new ideas. In *The Catalyst*, for example, Jeanne Liedtka, Robert Rosen, and Robert Wiltbank note that certain firms seem more capable of incremental innovation, others of transformative approaches, and some that simply won't do either until forced to by changing market conditions or angry shareholders. These last companies (and there are many of them) simply can't innovate because they are set in their ways and have no incentive to change.

A great example of utter resistance to engaging in innovation can be seen with much of the newspaper industry. Historically, most cities had many newspapers, but after several decades of consolidation, many papers enjoyed a local monopoly that discouraged innovation, even as the web began to pry the classifieds (which provided 40% or more of revenues) away from the newspapers. One newspaper publisher told us that he can't get anyone on the editorial side of the house to give anything more than lip service to innovation initiatives because, as he put it, "The team is in their 50s, don't believe that anything we can do will have any effect except to dumb down the content. So they're coasting 'til they can retire. After they do that, they can safely take potshots at us from the sidelines. It's happening all over. And meanwhile, readership keeps dropping."

CULTURAL ANTIBODIES IN ACTION

Several years ago, a major, profitable manufacturer of building materials engaged in a multi-year exercise to develop a new way of serving customers. The company, which provided products for new construction, recognized that an increasing percentage of the homes in the United States were, of course, not new, but needed to regularly replace the products this company already made. In a well-developed innovation process, the company first established an incubator far from corporate headquarters, so that the innovation team wouldn't be distracted. The process was well-funded and managed, and, over a period of many months, developed an entirely new way to make the company's products, specifically designed for existing homes, and, in the process, dramatically lowered their cost and created the opportunity for customization in a myriad of ways.

The company then tested these new products and discovered a huge demand in the marketplace. Excited by the possibilities, management began to introduce the new concept's key characteristics within the company. Almost at once, resistance began. Several divisions saw the innovation as a potential threat to existing profits, since the new manufacturing approach threatened to "cannibalize" existing market share. The new market opportunity, while appealing, was seen as less of a sure thing than the weakening of the existing market.

Top management persisted, and the new offerings brought in new revenues worth over $100 million. Even with this net increase in overall revenue, however, much of the company resisted the new line of products. At the same time, management felt that, now that the innovation was fully developed, it made sense to move its management away from the incubator and into corporate headquarters. Within a few years, the new innovations were significantly weakened in order to avoid the cannibalization that never came. In the end, the cultural antibodies largely destroyed the value of any innovation.

A Transformative Process

Unfortunately, relationship innovation is something that all companies need to do. In most cases, it's also a disruptive and transformative process. In writing this book, we looked at and experimented in our practices with a wide variety of ways to sidestep cultural antibodies and transform an organization at the same time. Unlike the walled-off approach of an incubator, we found that "becoming by doing" accomplishes both relationship innovation and the organizational change needed to support it over time.

Becoming by doing consists of six steps, which we call the six Ds:

- **Distancing.** In the first stage, set aside a specially structured team and pull yourself away from your own perspectives and biases. In this way, you can create new spaces, conceptual and organizational, for innovation to happen.

- **Discovering.** Next, research what your customers truly want from you at each stage of the relationship. Do this by charting their current experiences and comparing them to what customers really want and value. This step ends with waveline diagrams, but don't stop there. Uncover what your customers truly value and what kinds of changes will move the relationship from its current state to a better one.

- **Deciding.** At this point, conduct a strategic exercise to determine your plan of attack. Obviously, you will uncover many opportunities in the discovering phase and need to make choices as to what's practical and where your best opportunities for innovation lie. That way you can determine what to tackle first and what the resulting relationship should look like.

- **Declaring.** Even though nothing has been produced yet, you already align the organization around these new ideas and directions. This step generally involves creating a *relationship statement*, which updates the traditional brand positioning statement, and conducting a few short workshops. It's a short phase, but one that can't be overlooked. If you're making disruptive innovations that involve your customers, everyone who talks to or serves them will need to understand and communicate the new approach.

- **Designing.** In this phase, do what most organizations mean by innovation, which is sit down and design (or redesign) your touchpoints so that your customers can have the experiences they desire.

- **Delivering.** In the final stage, the rubber meets the road. You produce and implement the solution, not only for your customers, but also for your own people. You also maintain it over the long haul, ensuring that you deliver on your promises

Not all of these steps are created equal, of course. Designing and discovering will occupy the bulk of your innovation time, whereas distancing may require only part of a day. But all of the steps are important, and eliminating any one of them could upend your efforts. That's why we separate them out and discuss each one on its own.

EYE OPENERS

This chapter offers an overview of becoming by doing, the process we discuss in the rest of the book. It consists of six Ds, which are steps that help you not merely innovate, but also coordinate those innovation efforts across even a very large company. That way, you ensure that you're creating things that matter to your business, while getting everyone ready to deliver them. Some questions to think about:

- How does your company innovate?
- To what extent might your company be hostile to innovation, even though it says it is open to it?
- What kinds of changes would need to take place in your organization to innovate successfully around relationships?
- What have been your innovation successes and failures before now? What specific things aid or impede it within your organization?
- How must you prepare the organization for innovation—just as you prepare customers?

6

Distancing and Team Structure

This chapter will explore the first step of the relationship innovation process: distancing. Essentially, it involves setting up a team and giving team members distance or space for innovation. At the same time, it also requires gaining distance from their own personal biases and perceptions. Distancing is one of the shorter steps in the innovation process (it can take less than one day), but that doesn't make it any less crucial. If you fail to complete this step, you're likely to torpedo your chances for success before you even begin.

Team Structure and First Steps

Most innovation experts advocate for using small, nimble teams for the simple reason that they tend to be more effective and imaginative. Our approach goes against this grain. It advises that you break the process into two phases, one of which has a fairly large team, the second of which has a smaller, tighter core team.

For the larger team, select people from all departments and groups that impact innovation. The short list includes engineers, designers, marketers, PR, customer service, operations, and finance. The reason we want everyone on board is that relationship innovators need to work more broadly than is usual for such teams. Their efforts affect an entire organization, not merely resulting in a cool, new gadget. For that reason, draw representatives from as many relevant specializations as possible. That way, they can provide valuable perspectives that help innovate as well as foster close relationships among groups and evangelize the new ideas in their own home departments.

Usually, the larger team goes through the initial research phases of innovation. When it gets to the nuts and bolts of designing products and services, the team is pared down to a more traditional, smaller size. Even so, the larger team should still meet regularly with the core design team for updates. That way they can understand how things are progressing and report on any developments to the rest of the company.

A final point: the team must also be empowered. It should have support from and access to C-level leaders. That way, it can quickly communicate whatever it learns about customers' needs and desires to the people guiding the overall direction of the business.

Learning by Doing

The benefits of this tiered approach should be clear. As a team works together, a new culture naturally emerges among its members. The process of uncovering and making sense of new opportunities will, if done properly, encourage people to work in different ways. For example, they will do the following:

- Collaborate outside and across traditional silos.

- Build on each other's professional sensibilities to create new ways of thinking.

- Create a shared sense of empathy for each other as colleagues as well as customers.

- Produce greater openness to ambiguity and the process of quick concept refinement, balancing out existing tendencies toward standardization and predictable process.

- Bring learning and insight from the innovation team back into their own departments.

Not surprisingly, these ways of thinking and acting in companies are noted for their innovative culture. Collaborating, sharing, and empathizing typically help all organizations innovate better. The approach we're advocating simply offers a gentle but effective way of evolving corporate culture.

Preparing the Organization

At the same time the team creates distance, the rest of the business needs to give it space. Managers and other employees should be patient and understanding. Innovation takes time. They should also be open-minded. The solutions the team proposes may be highly unorthodox and defy accepted conventions. The best innovations will, necessarily, be disruptive—not only outside the company but inside as well. While the team works, the entire organization needs to prepare itself for the results.

Understanding the Problem of Biases

After you have a team physically set aside and isolated, the next step is to assist the team members in becoming aware of their biases and preconceptions and moving beyond them. Jared Spool, a well-respected user experience consultant, often tells a story of how badly biases can shape your understanding of your customers, and you might not even be aware of how many preconceptions and biases you have.

Jarod attended an introductory meeting with executives at an automotive company. He was tasked with explaining why they should consider studying their customers more deeply. Frankly, they were skeptical. They all drove cars built by the company and pored over customer research performed by others in the company. As a result, they thought they knew the customer experience pretty well.

Spool then asked them if any of them had bought a car recently. One executive said that he bought one the week before. Spool asked him how the process went. The executive explained that he went to a special office in the lobby of the building. He already knew everything about the cars and was able to submit a custom order, specifying what colors and options packages he wanted. The company then gave him a deep discount, and a few weeks later, his car magically appeared.

Spool's point was that this is nothing like how a customer buys a car. Most buyers do not shop for cars at their workplace. They don't receive big discounts, and they don't know every detail about a car long before it even hits the production line. They don't shop in a single place, and haven't driven the car before they start their car-buying search. The process for most people is one of education, consideration, familiarity, test drives, and agonizing over choices (and those are just the good parts). The executives thought they understood what it was like to be a customer, but they represented a tiny segment whose experiences and relationships were radically different from the rest.

In the distancing phase, you have to understand that you and your team members are never ordinary customers of your companies. You always belong to an unimportant and bizarre segment, whose experiences differ in fundamental ways from everyone else. Your experiences do not matter for innovation purposes. Neither do your impressions, hunches, and gut feelings—yet. You have to distance yourself from all that to start moving forward.

Recognizing Biases

To understand how to distance yourself from biases, here's a simple example from one of our colleagues. Brenda Laurel, a noted interactive and game designer and former chair of the Graduate Design Program at the California College of the Arts, often walks her students through an exercise that's excellent for doing this.

She gives her students a challenge, for which they are to design new solutions. This usually involves a specific customer segment (tweens, travelers, the elderly, and so on) and a seemingly contradictory theme (green luxury, for example). Then, before she allows the students to do a scrap of research, she makes them construct a detailed description of their potential customers. They have to write extensive profiles, collect photos from magazines, and even create scenarios about how those customers live their lives. All off the top of their heads.

After this, Brenda has the students post the results on the walls of a project room and present to their peers everything about their customers they believe. By doing this, she gets them to document their *preconceptions.* Their constructed customers reflect not research but their own biases. They have no basis in fact. They are simply hunches based on their general experiences. And they need to be acknowledged and forgotten.

When they are done, she asks the students to walk out and literally close the door behind them. Her process is to help them get those ideas out of their systems in order to be more open to insights they uncover

CASE STUDY: A BEAUTY COMPANY

To see how distancing can work in the real world, here's an example from Steve's work. A prominent consumer goods company came to his firm with an interesting question. What is beauty?

The company had a large range of products, from shampoo to dental floss. It considered all of them to be a natural fit for the beauty category. That said, they realized that they had no idea what *beauty* meant from an experiential point of view. Instead, they had a working assumption that products in that category helped people be more attractive.

Steve undertook an ethnographic project in the United States and China to see if there were patterns in how people experienced beauty. His team's theory going in was that beauty was an experience someone had in response to a stimulus, rather than an intrinsic characteristic of an object or process. In other words, beauty was more of a feeling than a quality. You could feel beautiful, but did not think of yourself as inherently beautiful or not.

That turned out to be true. The team uncovered a number of emerging beauty segments in both China and the United States that described how the beauty experience unfolded and how the touchpoints that evoked that experience differed from segment to segment.

in the field. When they finish their research, they can't claim that the insights they found were known all along, because the evidence of their biases is physically in front of them. Having one's biases so clearly laid out also helps sharpen the research insights, because every way they differ from what was uncovered during research becomes the basis for a new understanding.

Distancing is critical for relationship innovation. The elements of premium value—emotions, identity, and meaning—are less visible and more ethereal than things like price and product functionality.

The findings turned the conventional product category perspective on its head. Most women, for example, did not consider dental floss to be a beauty product. It was more about maintenance. On the other hand, detergent is not usually seen as a beauty product in the United States, but it is in China. The Chinese team learned that the swing of a golf club is beautiful—not because of the objects themselves, but what clubs and the golfer look like when they're in motion. They also learned that liquid pouring out of a bottle could pour beautifully or not. Beauty, in other words, is in the eye of very different types of beholders, and beholding, than is contemplated in conventional product category perspectives in the United States.

Next, it was time to help the company get some distance. Steve knew they didn't want to take up too much of their client's time, but wanted them to see things from this new perspective. So they built an installation that included museum banners at the front end, describing beauty experientially, and then, behind that, a series of small rooms. Each segment occupied a room, represented by videos of people from the research talking about what beauty felt like, as well as containing objects related to the experience.

A number of groups went through the installation to gain distance and perspective. Many returned to their departments with new insights. They rethought everything from products to packaging so that it better aligned with the desired beauty experience of the target markets.

Team-Based Distancing

Naturally, your team has to achieve what Laurel does with her students. Team members have to define everything they think they know up front. There are many ways to do this, and Laurel's is helpful. The important part is to state your biases and preconceptions up front. You should then clearly document your current beliefs about your customer relationship. That way, you can understand and set aside your own beliefs. This is especially useful if the research phase of innovation reveals those biases to be false, which it usually will.

EYE OPENERS

This chapter looks at the brief but crucial first step in the innovation process: distancing. The first step involves setting up a team; then the team states its biases and leaves them behind. This sets the stage for the next important phase, discovery. In it, you learn what your customers actually think and want—and where you have your best opportunities for innovation success.

Some food for thought:

- What do you think your company's relationship to its customers is?
- Do you believe you're correct, or would you be ready to admit you're not?
- How often would you say you try to distance yourself from preconceptions? If so, how?
- How close to your customers' lives do you live yours? How often do you experience life similarly?
- What kinds of things do you think you'd learn if you gained some perspective?

7

Discovering

After you recognize your biases and do your best to put them away, it's time to find the insights that will support better relationships. We call this the *discovering phase*. Anyone who has done design research or qualitative market insights should already be familiar with the structure of this process. The difference is that you'll be asking additional questions and looking for new insights.

The discovering phase results in a number of deliverables that serve as the foundation for design and innovation. They include your waveline diagram, which contains your customers' current experiences as well as the ones they want to have. In addition, you need to learn how to provide those better experiences. To do so, you also research what really matters to your customers. You uncover core meanings, or what customers truly value in their lives, independent of your offerings.

You determine what makes them tick and what kinds of creativity will trigger better experiences for them. You also need to understand how fast they want you to innovate, because if you move too fast or too slow, you can lose them.

Recognizing What You Don't Know

You saw in the last chapter how you could be wrong about your customers' experience. Of course, your impressions are not all you have to go on. You often have reams of data about your customers. Typically, this research divides your customers into different segments, with a range of demographic characteristics and attributes. It's fine to start with this kind of market data, but you need more. That's why discovering makes extensive use of qualitative research as well.

To understand why, this story from market insight expert Michael Perman offers a good example. In 2004, he was working as the senior director of Global Consumer Insights at Levi Strauss and Company. At the time, the company had uncovered an interesting fact about its customers. Although it had a premium brand and charged a considerable amount more for its products than its competitors, many of its customers were not affluent. Although they bought Levis, they weren't premium shoppers in other categories. In fact, they often couldn't really afford the jeans they were wearing.

Perman and his team interviewed a number people in this category across the country. One of them, whom we'll call Francine, lived with her two children in a trailer in a dusty stretch of Texas. Her home was an hour from the nearest Walmart, where she typically shopped for household and personal items she needed. Nonetheless, she would sometimes drive two hours to a fancier mall to buy Levis.

Francine isn't much of a sympathetic consumer. She barely gets by on what she makes. In fact, her Levis are, in a very real sense, taking food out of her kids' mouths. As a result, she might appear to be a typical "welfare mom" derided by commentators on TV, taking our tax dollars to fund a frivolous lifestyle.

Nothing could be further from the truth. Francine impressed Perman and his team from the moment they set foot in her modest but well-kempt home. They learned that she held two jobs and was acutely aware that she was barely getting by. She scrimped and saved on everything and had a laser focus on making a better life for her children. When asked why she would drive so far out of her way and pay so much more so that she and her kids could wear Levi's brand jeans, she had a surprising answer: "Because I don't want my children growing up thinking that they're poor... [and] that they can't achieve more in their lives."

Francine wasn't vain or impractical. She knew how brutal children could be to one another. She knew that clothes mattered immensely, even if they shouldn't. She tried hard to give her children a better future, and part of that included how their peers treated them and, more importantly, how they thought about themselves and their opportunities. The last thing she wanted was for them to believe that they were poor kids who would never amount to much.

Perman and team were deeply moved. Through further research, they found that Francine was representative of a broad and real segment of the company's customers, one that no one had ever thought about. They gained a profound insight into the kind of company Levi Strauss needed to be and the special relationship it had with people like Francine. She reminded them that Levis had to be the company she felt it was.

If distancing involves recognizing and forgetting biases, discovering is a journey into the unknown. Merely looking at the data, it would appear that Francine's customer segment was short-sighted and irresponsible. Qualitative research, however, revealed it to be forward looking and inspirational. To be successful at innovation, you need to know the truth.

Uncovering State of Mind

Discovering does not move in a linear fashion. It is a research process designed to uncover multiple insights at once. Rather than looking at the current waveline first, then the desired waveline, then core meanings, the typical method is to undergo a series of exercises with customers that reveal all of these—or parts of them—at the same time. It's a process more akin to holographic, rather than hierarchical sets of data: each piece describes a bit of all the others.

Where do you find your customers? As we've said before, customers develop a relationship with you through experiences over time. As a result, you have to look at the time span of your engagement with them and make sure that you interview people at key points in that journey. For example, imagine you're researching the relationship a person has with his or her smartphone, and you know, on average, that your customers own a smartphone for about two years. In such a case, you might want to interview people who are:

- Thinking about getting a new phone
- Actively looking
- Recent purchasers
- Owners for a month
- Owners for six months
- Owners for a year

With this information, you can assemble a snapshot of your relationship with your customers and their experiences of you over time.

Don't break your customers into segments at this point and research each independently. Rather, identify segments *while* you are in the research phase. Learn how they are experiencing your offerings. If some experience them differently from others, use that information to help identify segments. This process is described in detail later in this chapter.

Researching Experiences and Relationships

It would be great, at this point, if you could just grab a bunch of customers, ask them what their experiences were and what they wanted from you, and get right to solutions. Unfortunately, it's not that easy. People are rarely able to give you an accurate account of why something matters to them or how it engages them in a meaningful way. Market researchers have long understood that most people are not very good at articulating such things. For example, few people can remember accurately how they felt in the past or predict how they will feel and act in the future.

Some have used this information to argue that customer research is a waste of time. But just because your customers aren't great about describing what's meaningful in their lives doesn't mean the info is not there—or that it's not extremely powerful. It merely tells you that experience is difficult to uncover and understand.

Instead, use indirect and open-ended methods. There are a wide range of these, but the five most effective include:

- Metaphor
- Semiotic analysis
- Role-play
- Laddering
- Empathy through simple interactions

Metaphor

To understand how metaphor works, imagine that you decide to climb Mount Washington in New Hampshire. Depending on your level of fitness, this could be either an impossible dream or a walk in the park. Now imagine that the first thing you see as you crest the hill is a researcher in a white lab coat. She sits you down at a table and spreads out three pictures. One depicts an Olympic runner crossing a finish line, another shows a woman comforting a child, and a third shows a gavel in a courtroom. She then asks you which one represents how you feel.

The three are obviously metaphors for feelings, and they're easy to interpret. The gavel is about justice, the runner about triumph, and the woman about comfort, or even harmony.

You might think that most people would choose the Olympic runner because of their sense of accomplishment in scaling the mountain. But, believe it or not, a substantial group of people will identify with the woman comforting the child. The reason is that the experience of climbing a hill was difficult and unpleasant for them, and they now need a hug. Even more oddly, a substantial group will choose the gavel. The reason is that they've spent time in a natural setting and feel they've done the right thing by getting back to nature. The contemplation of the wrongness of how people treat the environment will awaken their sense of justice.

Metaphors offer a shortcut into peoples' states of mind. Although many find it difficult to articulate how they feel in words, it's easier for them to choose a picture or two that captures the essence of their experience. Of course, metaphorical investigation does require the researcher to interpret, and researchers can make mistakes. But with a little experience, you can become very good at understanding why people choose the pictures they do—especially combined with other methods.

Metaphors can offer four different kinds of insight:

1. They help describe the experiences customers have at particular points of time.

2. They can be used before customers encounter significant touchpoints to see what, if any, change has taken place.

3. They can help convey overall feelings during particular phases of interaction, such as when someone is shopping for versus using something.

4. They also help construct the current and desired wavelines for customer experience.

One important caveat: the metaphors that you use for this sort of work will always need to be rooted in the relevant culture. In Steve's firm's study of beauty, for example, the team started by using the same images representing different types of meaningful experiences in both the United States and China. This turned out to be a mistake and, in retrospect, an obvious one. The metaphors were correct for the States, but virtually every one of them was wrong in China. For a basic example, if you want to use a visual metaphor in China for "freedom," a picture of a bald eagle soaring above a mountain landscape doesn't work, not least because the bird doesn't exist there. Of course, Steve's team wasn't that ham-fisted in its choices, but they did realize quickly that they needed to localize more of the metaphors that made better sense to those customers.

Semiotic Analysis

Another useful tool for understanding state of mind is directly tied to the form and packaging of a product and the words used to describe it. This is known as "semiotics," and, technically speaking, it's the study of signs and symbols.

This sounds a lot more abstract and complex than it is. To see how it works, you merely need to think about your favorite *eco* or sustainable product, such as an environmentally friendly shampoo. There is a good chance it comes in natural-looking materials like cardboard or bamboo. It likely has chunky or hand-drawn lettering and some kind of green in its packaging. It may even seem handmade or deliberately underdesigned. In addition, the language used to describe it will generally contain concrete nouns ("Unisys" and "Revent" would not qualify).

The following figure shows three examples of eco-friendly logos to illustrate the point.

It's no accident that these products all seem to come from a similar place. Each has green somewhere, the lettering is either idiosyncratic or casual, and the words are concrete and simple. That's because, even if you don't recognize them consciously, you have your own embedded cultural coding for the eco category. Its products do not look like construction products. Boxes for high-end shoes look quite different from the ones you get at a discount store. Chinese restaurants in the United States used to always have paper lanterns, Year of the Animal calendars, red tablecloths, and faux Chinese typefaces. All of those things coded for "Chinese" to us in a more naïve time, even though they didn't necessarily feature prominently in China itself. These stereotypes, today, can be offensive to the people they are meant to represent. Humans have a shared understanding of what certain kinds of products are supposed to look like—and that, in turn, can uncover your expectations of what you want from a company and how you interpret it.

ENLIGHTENMENT

In the United States, a picture of someone meditating is typically used to symbolize enlightenment. For the Chinese, however, the lotus is a more appropriate symbol of enlightenment.

Semiotic analysis is especially useful in uncovering what are known as *triggers*. You can think of triggers as building blocks for the experiences your customers have of your offerings. For example, a trigger could be colors and words that produce specific associations in your customers' minds. They can also be flavors or aromas. In the United States, "clean" is often associated with bleach, pine, or mint scents. Thus, cleaning products tend toward these smells to signal "clean" and reassure customers that their items and objects are now dirt free. Elsewhere, however, different scents say "clean." In Europe, it's often herbs, like basil or chamomile.

Semiotic analysis also helps create better advertising, messaging, and the shape, materials, packaging, or other characteristics of a product or service. In addition, it can be used to help convey the current relationship (their current waveline) and what customers might want (their desired waveline). It also identifies the elements from which you can choose in the design phase that may or may not work better at communicating important aspects of the experience.

Recognize that symbols may vary between segments and are constantly evolving. After all, most of us don't expect to find a placemat for the Year of the Dog at serious Chinese restaurants anymore.

Role-Play

Role-play offers a great way to understand the experiences that customers have with your organization, as well as the ones they want over time. As with semiotics, this technique involves presenting different customers with different types of interaction. For example, imagine you had a hotel chain and hired a researcher with improvisational, role-playing experience to determine the aspects of a great check-in experience. In a typical scenario, she would gather a representative sample of your target audience. She would then ask them to play the role of customers, while she acted as the hotel clerk at the front desk.

The trick is that she would vary her approach with different people. Some she'd treat exactly as the hotel chain currently did. With others, she might be chatty or taciturn. She could greet them by discussing the weather or instead remark on something going on that weekend ("Are you here for the fair?"). After the customers had completed the fake check-in process, she would then ask them to describe their reactions. That would allow her to understand the kinds of experiences they valued.

Role-play is particularly valuable for service businesses or any situation where customers interact directly with a company.

Laddering

Laddering is a technique for uncovering what people truly value, both from us and in general. The technique is based on a single question: "And what does that do for you?" For example, imagine you work for a company that sells pens and pencils, and you want to know what a particular pen means to someone. In a typical laddering exercise, you might ask him to show you his favorite pen. Then you would ask "And what does that do for you?"

The first answer you get is usually functional. The person will say something about how it allows him to write things down. Then you ask again, "And what does that do for you?" That usually ups the ante and forces him to respond more deeply. For example, he might say it helps him to write down thoughts and ideas so he doesn't forget them. Ask the question again, and you might find out that pens make him confident that he won't forget things that his children need. Eventually, you might learn that he really values being confident that he's being a good parent.

At this point, you've identified something that truly matters to him: being a confident parent. It's possible that that insight could give you a direction for innovative thinking. You could design a special pad that adheres to the pen to increase that confidence, or make a more reliable pen, or one that writes under bad weather conditions. You could certainly target him with messaging based on confidence, rather than utility. But thanks to laddering, you have insight into what he truly values.

Other laddering exercises don't involve a physical object or even your own business's offerings. For example, imagine your home is on fire. Your kids, pets, family, and friends are not there, so you don't have to worry about them. Your possessions are another matter, though. In fact, you have time to save only one thing. Which one do you choose? When you answer, drill down and ask "What does that do for you" until you uncover something that is essential to you.

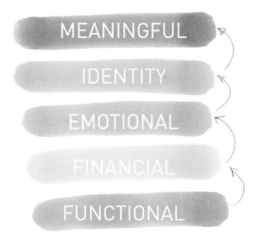

Empathy Through Simple Interactions

For whatever reason, the simplest technique often elicits the most resistance: empathy. It is, of course, not necessarily scientific, but that doesn't make it less important. Relying on empathy to make sense of what someone is going through is often the best way to gain deep insights into how to help them.

Good empathetic work involves having an open heart in conversations with customers. In order to understand what matters to them, you have to be willing to be vulnerable and transparent about what matters to you, just as you would if you were trying to understand a friend's challenges in life. In addition, empathy requires you to ask open-ended questions that give respondents ample opportunity to express their feelings. That is easier for most people than answering your laddering questions. But, if you add the insights you gain from empathetic inferences to those from the other techniques we've mentioned, you should be able to arrive at an accurate understanding of what people want most to happen in their lives when they use a product or service.

Intensity

If you interview different customers across their timelines, you should be able to get a good idea of what experiences they're having with you and when. You can chart interest, disappointment, elation, boredom, and many other things. But your waveline diagrams also contain something else: intensity. The reason is easy to see. A mild sense of boredom is not the same as an intense sense of boredom. A minor sense of wonder is not really all that important, whereas Disneyland-style wonder gives a huge boost to a relationship.

BEYOND TWO-BY-TWO THINKING

Business analysts today love two-by-two grids. The following figure shows a two-by-two grid for soft drinks. On the horizontal axis, you can find taste (however that's defined) and on the vertical axis, price. The dots show where all of the companies rate on both.

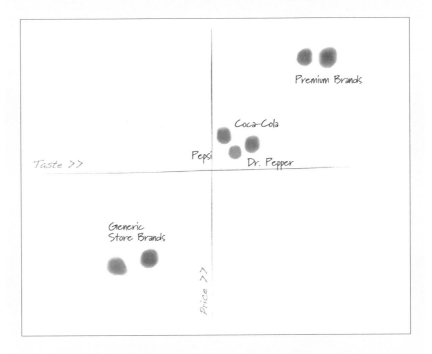

Grids like this have their place. They can make it easy to identify market opportunities and see where you rank against your peers. That said, they have a narrow range of assumptions that can lead you astray. This one, for example, would seem to indicate that high-priced brands of soda are able to charge a much larger premium than Coke and Pepsi, even though they taste only slightly better. It would seem, then, that by a slight improvement in taste, Coke could reap big rewards.

sidebar continues on next page

BEYOND TWO-BY-TWO THINKING (continued)

Obviously, this is wrong. Coke and Pepsi do a wonderful job in fostering their relationships with customers, which drives considerable loyalty and longer-term value. Although the premium brands in this example seem to be driving greater value, they're probably responding to health trends or speaking to the snobbery of a niche audience. Most of them will be short-lived, as customers will move on to cheaper brands or the next big thing.

For another example, the next figure takes a look at a typical segmentation for theme parks.

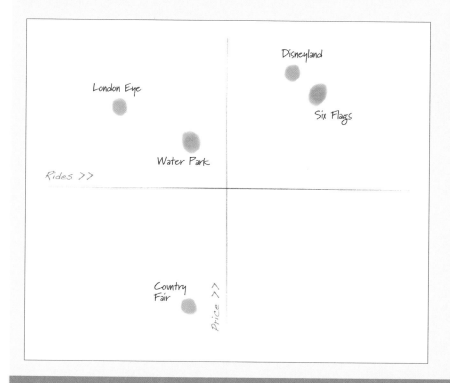

This example shows how a simple price/performance diagram fails to account for the strength of a relationship. Disneyland, it appears, costs a good deal more than Six Flags, even though it offers fewer rides. That may be true, but it obscures the reason why, which is that Disney invests much more heavily in providing wonder. The number of rides is a functional indicator (and a poor one) of the quality of a relationship.

Of course, two-by-two grids are not merely problematic when the axes represent only basic values (like price and performance). They're also problematic simply because they reduce the conversation down to two things, when there are likely many more relevant ones. Discovering usually uncovers four or five critical issues in a relationship, all of which need to be accounted for in your strategic thinking (even though they're more difficult to represent in a chart than two).

There are a number of techniques for understanding intensity, the simplest of which involves a number or color-coding system. To understand how it works, think about your experience on a roller coaster ride. Pretty much, you're mainly going to experience excitement. But that feeling will vary over time as you oscillate between terrifying drops and less scary ones, uphill stretches of relief, and short bursts of exciting speed.

To figure out your intensity, you simply use a device that allows you to select a number at any time between 1 and 5. Five is ultra-high excitement; 1 is low excitement. And 2, 3, and 4 lie in between. The device might also track additional data, like the loudness of your screams or the tightness of your grip on the safety bar.[1] This information establishes intensity fairly quickly and enables you to chart it on a waveline diagram for the ride.

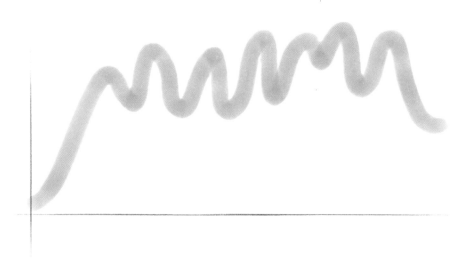

1. Not far in the future, we should be able to measure intensity even more accurately by tracking things like heart rate and the amount of adrenaline pumping through your body.

It gets slightly trickier when you look at the desired waveline—or what customers want from an experience. If you ask people what kind of experiences they'd like to have on a roller coaster, many will answer "really intense" the whole time. But you know that's not right. As much as riders may think that an all-excitement rollercoaster ride would be ideal, they would probably not like it as much as a more varied experience crafted to build and release tension over the course of the ride.

In that case, you have to explore customers' past experiences and compare the descriptions of other rides they enjoyed in order to understand their expectations and what might really work for them. You could also look at excitement intensity in other areas of their lives. For example, if you ask about their favorite game or film, you might gain insight into the experiences they desire.

A number of additional techniques can also help you establish intensity. These include market testing, observing people using a product, or building prototypes and allowing people to interact with them. None of these techniques are perfect by themselves, but all provide some insight to what customers want. In fact, you often need to triangulate it from the different techniques, using several to establish the facts.

Segmenting by Experience

As mentioned earlier, you don't typically segment customers up front, but rather allow the segments to emerge during research. To see why, look at a discovering exercise done by a group of Nathan's students involving a study of jury duty in San Francisco. You might think that most people would find jury duty a negative experience: a tedious, unwanted interruption in their lives. And, yes, the students certainly found plenty of people who felt that way.

Surprisingly, however, they also uncovered something else: a significant number of people who were interested in and curious about the process. Although their lives were disrupted, they nonetheless wondered what a trial was like and hoped to get chosen to serve on a jury (so long as it didn't take up too much time). A final set of people combined the two: they were interested in jury duty, but knew it was also a hassle they should probably avoid.

The students gave those segments these names: the Irritated, the Interested, and the Conflicted. The Interested wanted experiences quite different from the Irritated. They were much less annoyed by the waiting, intrigued by the *voir dire* questioning, and curious about what kind of case they might hear. The Conflicted, of course, shared the interest in the process but also the dread of getting chosen. Obviously, if you wanted to improve the jury duty experience for these groups, you'd have to treat them differently. In the figure, the lower line represents the "current" experience and the upper line the "ideal" experience.

CURRENT vs IDEAL

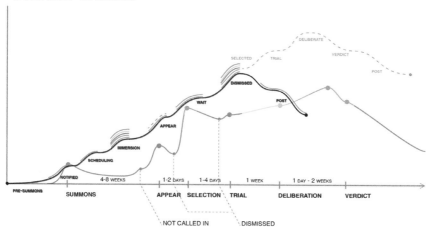

NEW JOURNEY MAP

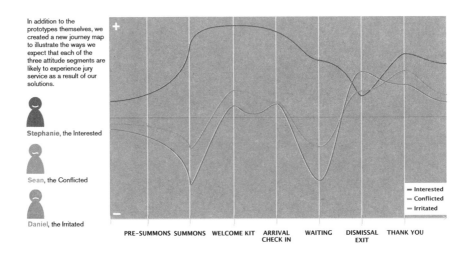

In addition to the prototypes themselves, we created a new journey map to illustrate the ways we expect that each of the three attitude segments are likely to experience jury service as a result of our solutions.

Stephanie, the Interested

Sean, the Conflicted

Daniel, the Irritated

— Interested
— Conflicted
— Irritated

PRE-SUMMONS SUMMONS WELCOME KIT ARRIVAL CHECK IN WAITING DISMISSAL EXIT THANK YOU

Whenever there are significant differences in customers' experience of the same thing, they can be divided into segments. Sometimes, these segments conform to your expectations or to traditional segmentation methods, but usually not. It would be difficult to predict a person's experience of jury duty based solely on his or her age, gender, income, ZIP code, or profession.

Instead, it's better to look for patterns in the experiences that customers value in your business or brand—or patterns of behavior they display—and make those your segments. Whenever you find significant differences in experience between groups, you know you need to construct different waveline diagrams for each—and possibly innovate independently for each.

More on Demographics

You may encounter resistance about demographics from more traditional clients initially. They'd prefer to use the same demographic data that everyone uses. Demographics are seductive, because they are easy to derive and seem to be hard and tangible. However, they are not necessarily as tangible as you may think. They tend to be based on biases and conceal qualitative experience, which plays a more important role in creating a long-term relationship and building premium value.

For example, you probably know of a kind of person often called an "experience traveler." They pride themselves on seeking-out interesting and unique experiences wherever they go. You won't find them on a cruise or hitting a water park. They'll rarely be found in a chain restaurant. Instead, they're interested in going to obscure places and having authentic experiences. They might spend their winter vacation taking drumming classes in Japan. Or they could take a road trip through North Carolina, where they seek out obscure barbecue joints. They might eat at the best restaurant in town one night and at an up-and-coming food truck the next. If you tried to segment them using demographics, their behavior would not conform to the expectations of income, age, profession, and gender. Nonetheless, they are a growing, recognized, and one of the most valuable segments in the travel industry today.

One last point on segmentation: you can segment endlessly, but typically your budget is only going to allow you to innovate on a certain number of segments. You should only segment as much as your innovation budget can support—otherwise, you're gaining insights that you can't use.

Making Dynamic Personas

After you have segments, there's an additional task to do: create dynamic personas, fictional characters that represent the segments you uncover and the very real insights you have about them. You do this for two reasons. The first is that human beings, including designers, engineers, and other innovators, are much better at remembering and integrating information when it's told as a story. The second is that having a persona reminds you that you're not developing for yourself and your own preferences. You're doing this for your customers.

In creating personas, you have any number of options for content. Focus on a few things to ensure that you capture what the segment truly values and what kinds of experience its members want. Typically, include all of the following:

- **Who they are.** Describe them and how they see themselves. This includes their careers as well as their personal and social lives, and what a typical day in each might look like.

- **What they love.** Know what is meaningful to them. Describe their core meanings, values, and how they interact with whatever category of product or service you're trying to innovate for.

- **How they behave.** For this, explore how they interact with your offerings (and each other), what paths they take to purchase and use, and how it all makes them feel. This might include data from actual transactions or customer service logs, as well as your own observations.

- **What they want.** This encompasses all of the things they wish their lives could be (and how your offerings might help achieve these).

Bringing Personas to Life

As with segments, personas have a long history in market research and innovation. But, like many old things, they're due for an upgrade. We advocate creating rich ones that are alive and responsive to changing tastes and times.

We do this largely by using social media. For example, a persona's music preferences are often important. (Music preferences can be a big part of someone's identity and a great identifier of similarities with others.) But, if you're trying to describe a persona with cutting-edge taste, you have a problem. Any song you pick to illustrate this will likely go out of style long before your persona gets used. Luckily, there is a great way to get around that. Rather than continually updating a persona with musical preferences, you can create a web page for her and have her follow a few cutting-edge Spotify lists or Twitter feeds that are dynamically fed into her profile.[2]

Another, more in-depth way to keep the persona alive is to put up fake pages on LinkedIn or Facebook for them and update the pages with relevant cultural information as time goes on. This not only helps to keep the persona fresh, but it also serves to remind you that people are dynamic and that you should expect their preferences to change over time. Someone on the research team can be assigned the responsibility to constantly refresh and update these profiles with the latest information so that designers, engineers, and others on the team can easily check them whenever they need and have access to the most current insights.

Opportunity Spaces

When you understand segments, reactions at different points, and their intensity, you have all the building blocks you need to create your current and desired wavelines. Plot the experiences for each segment

---

2. For more on dynamic personas, visit www.dynamicpersonas.com.

across time into a waveline diagram, adding in any phases of engagement that you have seen. That gives you a visual representation of the experiences your customers have with you—and want to have.

At this point, you should be able to identify spaces that offer the best innovation opportunities. The easiest way to do so is to simply look at current and desired wavelines and find the biggest gaps between them.

Consumer Experience Waveline

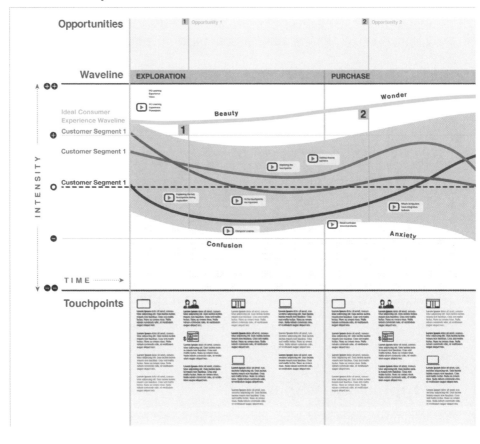

A second way to identify opportunities is to draw general conclusions about which experiences would be worthwhile to shift across multiple touchpoints and across time. For example, let's look again at the waveline diagram representing customer experiences buying and using tablet PCs. On it, at the very bottom, you can easily see specific opportunities uncovered, against which they devoted their innovation efforts.

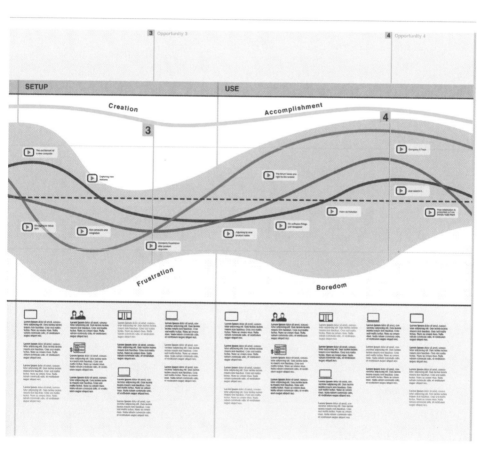

Beyond Waveline Diagrams

Discovering doesn't end with waveline diagrams. In addition to understanding relationships, you also need to know how to improve them. To do so, collect insights that give you a deeper understanding of the customer. Essentially, this consists of four elements:

- **Core meanings:** The building blocks of the most premium type of value

- **Triggers:** Sensory attributes that trigger associations in customers (especially of meaning and identity)

- **Pace:** The right timing that moves the experience in accordance with preferences

- **Design principles:** The guiding attributes of any product or service you create to support the relationship

Core Meanings

As you know, laddering exercises are great at uncovering things that people truly value or make life worth living, called core meanings. In *Making Meaning,* Nathan and Steve identified 15 of these, although there may be a couple more. The best way to understand them is by looking at their definitions.

- **Accomplishment:** Some companies succeed in giving people a sense of accomplishment. A good example is American Express, whose cards, which have high balances and must be paid off every month, give people the feeling that they've made it in life.

- **Beauty:** This is the appreciation of qualities that give pleasure to the senses or spirit. Of course, beauty is in the eye of the beholder and thus highly subjective, but the desire for it is ubiquitous. Everyone aspires to beauty in all that surrounds them, from architecture and fine furnishing to clothing and cars.

- **Community:** Many companies are great at making you feel like you belong to a club. Harley Davidson, for example, is phenomenally successful partly because its motorcycles define their owners as rebels and a tribe apart. This is meaningful to them. Similarly, America's NASCAR circuit (or any sports team for that matter) makes its fans feel like they belong to something bigger than themselves.

- **Creation:** Here is the sense of having produced something new and original, and in so doing, making a lasting contribution. Creation is what makes "customizable" seem like a desirable attribute, rather than more work for the buyer—for example, making the salad bar a pleasure rather than a chore.

- **Duty:** Some companies deal in moral or ethical issues, thus making their customers feel as if they are fulfilling a duty they have to the world. When you buy fair trade coffee or environmentally responsible cleansers, you're doing the right thing. That has positive meaning for you.

- **Enlightenment:** A clear understanding through logic or inspiration is not limited to those who meditate and fast. It is a core expectation of offerings from news sources, too.

- **Freedom:** The sense of living without unwanted constraints often plays tug-of-war with the desire for security; more of one tends to decrease the other. Nevertheless, freedom is enticing, whether it's freedom from dictators or red tape.

- **Harmony:** The balanced and pleasing relationship of parts to a whole is desired, whether in nature, society, or an individual. When we seek a work/life balance, we are in pursuit of harmony.

- **Justice:** The assurance of equitable and unbiased treatment is the sense of fairness and equality that underlies the concept of "everyman" or "average Joe."

- **Oneness:** This is a sense of unity with everything around us. It is what some seek from the practice of spirituality and what others expect from a good tequila. Although we don't normally think of them as a company, the Grateful Dead sustained its revenues for decades building an experience that connected with its fans' desire for oneness.

- **Redemption:** This is the atonement or deliverance from past failure or decline. Though this might seem to stem from negative experiences, the impact of the redemptive experience is highly positive. Like community and enlightenment, redemption has a basis in religion, but it also applies to any sensation that delivers us from a less desirable condition to another, more pleasing, one that can be redemptive.

- **Security:** The freedom from worry about loss has been a cornerstone of civilization; in the United States, in particular, a sense of security acquired increased meaning and relevance after 9/11. Security encompasses safety and applies to loved ones as well as personal possessions.

- **Truth:** Truth is a commitment to honesty and integrity, and it underlies everything from Whole Foods to Newman's Own, both of which portray themselves as upright and candid. It's hard for companies to maintain truth, but it's an extremely important and valuable meaning for some (and especially young) people.

- **Validation:** This is the recognition of oneself as a valued individual worthy of respect. Every externally branded piece of clothing counts on the attraction of this meaningful experience whether it's Ralph Lauren Polo or Old Navy, as does any other brand with status identification as a core value.

- **Wonder:** Sometimes we just want to be overwhelmed with amazement. Las Vegas, with its over-the-top shows and storybook casinos, often accomplishes this (while taking our money in the process).

You can find a more detailed discussion of meaning in a book Nathan and Steve wrote earlier, *Making Meaning* (New Riders, 2006); you can also find a list of core meanings at that book's website at www.makingmeaning.org.

Triggers

In the discussion of semiotics earlier in this chapter, you saw that signs, symbols, words, and design elements could evoke different reactions in our audiences. As part of the discovering phase, you need to learn what the right triggers are, so you can incorporate them into your solutions, as needed.

For example, as mentioned earlier, the color green—or certain shades of it anyway—triggers a connection to nature for many people. That's great if it aligns with the experience you're trying to establish. Of course, it's terrible if your touchpoint is trying to evoke something else—say, precision or accomplishment.

It's worth pointing out that, as with metaphors, triggers are culturally determined. The Japanese like interfaces with a lot of elements, whereas Europeans tend to prefer lots of white space. In Korea and China, white is the color of death. In the West, it signals elegance and purity. You have to determine what communicates what to your particular audiences. You wouldn't want to design a wedding invitation in white for a Korean audience, or one in black for a Western audience. Each would trigger the wrong associations.

The same is true for many other design decisions. Numbers trigger superstitions in most cultures (but different ones in different cultures). Sound designers are experts in crafting music or film scores to trigger specific emotions during a song or film. Chefs constantly experiment with different flavor combinations but always with an understanding of what these will trigger for diners. Even price can trigger different connotations. Most people buy wine by price, for example. In a store, they're likely to narrow their choices first by price (in relation to the most and least expensive offered), independent of any other data, and then likely choose based on the design of the label. If the wine is more expensive, that triggers an assumption of its quality, regardless of whether this is true.

The important thing is to discover and document which triggering elements you need to innovate for premium value.

Pace

You also need to understand your customers' appetite for change. This helps determine both how different touchpoints should be designed, as well as how often you should change them. To understand why this is important, think about how differently children and older people view change. The elderly often complain about new things and having to learn about new technologies or processes. Kids are usually the opposite. They can't wait for the next software update or new version of their favorite Xbox game.

These are extremes (and stereotypes), of course, but people typically have a preferred pace for change across different experiences and contexts. A person with a headache wants change immediately, whereas a person enjoying a massage wants the experience to last as long as possible. Some software users may want an update every 6 months; others don't want to see change for 12, 18, or more.

People always have a preference for the pace of interaction and change. In your discovering phase, it is a crucial element that helps you determine:

- The opportunities you have for innovation
- The pace of your interactions
- How frequently you should innovate to get there

UNDERSTANDING PACE THROUGH GAMING

We can understand pace with a fun example: massive, multiplayer, online, role-playing games. In these games, which are often based around *Lord of the Rings*-type worlds, you typically select a role from seven to ten archetypes. You might be a warrior or a wizard, a scout or a big dumb guy who can crush things. You then join other players in a team or a guild and set forth on adventures together. As you become more skilled, you rise to higher levels, moving to a new part of the game with harder challenges and tougher competition.

Designers of such games are acutely aware that their players have an infinite number of ways they can navigate the game—not least because their experience partly depends on the other individuals on their teams. In addition, some will take on individual quests and challenges, whereas others will stick to a team. Wizards have a different interaction with the game than orcs. Big dumb guys who can crush things do not solve problems in the same way as dwarfs. Still, game designers have to construct a journey that's compelling, no matter what path people take and with what identity.

Over time, the gaming industry has realized that success depends on how the players experience changes during play. They have built-in expectations about how hard it should be to master a level. Too easy, and they get bored. Too difficult, and they get frustrated. A level also only holds interest for so long, and something new has to come along to keep the players engaged.

In fact, around 2011, a Microsoft user-experience designer named Ryan Opina conducted an exhaustive review of successful practices in such games. In it, he identified a number of stages that every good game has to provide, irrespective of the story the game tells:

- **Entry:** Everything is new and exciting as the player starts a game. That said, she can be easily frustrated if she's killed off too soon, or things are too hard.

- **Practice:** The player learns the basics and progresses through the challenges. She has a sense of where she wants to be and is heading toward that goal.

- **Mastery:** The player is at the more difficult stages of the game. It might mean that she has now reached a high level with her team. They can go alone on high-level activities or compete one-on-one with other master-level players.

- **Burn-out:** The player feels like she's done everything she can in the game. She gets bored with the same experiences, and, oddly enough, may dread the social obligations she feels toward her team. The fun seems to be gone.

- **Recovery:** Hopefully, the player gets past boredom and finds pleasure in occasional play. She may do casual things for fun, join friends on occasion, but she may never play with the same intensity she once did.

In other words, when designing such a game, you have to make sure that the right pacing is available at the right times. The designer doesn't dictate the path that players take, but instead ensures that the path has a certain structure of difficulty and achievement. In addition, when the first wave of hardcore players gets comfortable in the recovery stage, the games should probably release new levels and features. Or the company might release an entirely new game—or, at least, build expectations for it.

HEADSPACE

In 1993, musician Thomas Dolby created a company, Headspace, to develop a music engine for computer games. His company invented a cinema-quality soundtrack that could be created on the fly, responding to the action of the game. If the player was in a learning or exploration mode, the soundtrack would consist of different melodies than if they were traveling or in battle. Likewise, the rhythm of the music would pick up with faster players and slow down with slower behavior. In other words, it was a responsive soundtrack that made a significant difference in the experience of the game. Although this engine didn't catch on, the principle is the same as what's being describing with pace: you need to be responsive to your customer's experience in real time.

ELEMENTS OF PACING

To create a good understanding of your customers' pace, you need to determine two things: the speed at which the touchpoint unfolds, and the frequency at which changes occur.

Speed

Think of this as action over time. If you go to a McDonald's drive-thru, you expect things to happen fast—in less than five minutes, typically. The problem McDonald's faces is that a drive-thru is linear and only one person can pay at a time. At busy times, it's hard for cashiers to physically keep up with the customers' pace. To do so, McDonald's has led a wave of innovation in drive-thrus. First, it offered two windows to drivers, one where they pay, and another where they pick up their food. More recently, the company has designed intelligent systems where cars can order at one of two stations. The traffic is then merged so that the staff always delivers the right order to the right person.

In this way, the company works hard to keep the pace right, even at the busiest time.

Pacing is easily understood in film media, so perhaps an example here might make it most clear. Consider the difference in pacing between two different action-adventure films, *Transformers III* from 2011 and *Goldfinger* from 1964. Yes, the two films have slightly different audiences (though much overlap), and yes they're from different eras—and that's the point. Some audiences expect and even prefer the pace of change in experiences to be very different. Anything else and it doesn't feel quite right. It's up to us to understand how customers react and what would be successful for them.

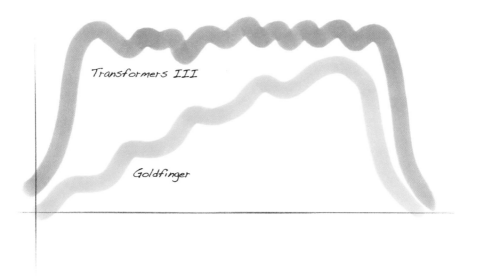

Speed is relatively easy to uncover during discovery, either through role-play or direct observation.

Frequency

Think of this as change over time. There's an old saying that states that change is constant, and that companies must always evolve rapidly to keep ahead of a disruptive landscape. Innovation studies are often predicated on the idea that you must innovate as quickly as possible. As Eric Schmidt of Google once said about Microsoft, if you don't capitalize on every innovation wave in technology, you're in trouble.[3]

Your customers probably disagree. A constant increase in the pace of change can overwhelm and depress some customer segments. Faster innovation can also lead to faster obsolescence—and waste. Your customers may not like waste. Besides, you don't actually need to be first to be successful. Most organizations would be better off focusing on delivering the right thing at the right time. Even a company as seemingly innovative as Apple did not invent the mp3 player, the smartphone, or the tablet. But it launched better products at the right time, when everyone already had some familiarity with the basic concepts of how they worked.

What is the right pace of change for your customers? Whatever your research uncovers about their needs and tolerance for change. Even if you know what your customers want from innovation, you also have to contend with their adaptability to accept and integrate new things. You may be able to get to your desired waveline, or relationship, pretty quickly. But if you do so through a jarring transition rather than step-by-step, you may lose everyone.

One way of thinking about the problem is to determine where your customers sit on the innovation curve. The tech industry, for example, has long identified several types of customers, but especially those on different ends of the spectrum: early adopters and laggards. Early adopters are people who can adapt quickly to new offerings they

3. *Barron's,* June 20, 2011, p. 18.

perceive might meet their needs and desires. Most are tolerant of integration or compatibility issues, because they like a fast pace of change. Many of them even believe that being on the "cutting edge" is a part of their identity.[4]

Laggards, on the other hand, want to use an offering without having to pay attention to it. They don't want to learn anything new or difficult or have their lives disrupted. They just want it to work exactly as it already does. They don't *like* change. These are hard people to please with innovation. Luckily, they're also not great in number. Most are somewhere in the middle and don't need or seek the latest and greatest, but aren't the last to adopt, either.

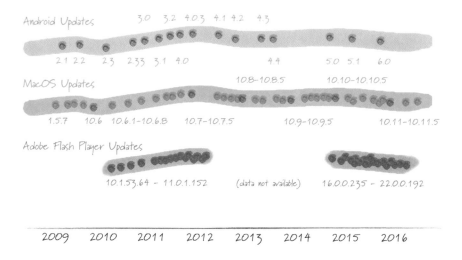

The important part is to figure out where your customers sit on the spectrum and to structure your innovation efforts accordingly.

4. This tendency among early adopters to be easily bored is underappreciated in the literature but key to the buying behavior. See Peter Toohey, *Boredom*, Yale University Press, 2011, p. 15, for more, particularly relating to "tedium" caused by too much predictability and sameness.

Design Principles

The final task is to document and bundle all of these insights together for those who will develop new solutions. At this point, you create one final deliverable: a set of design principles that ensure that any concepts you generate deliver on the experiences people want to have. This is not as difficult as it sounds. Broadly speaking, you need only five to seven principles to guide the development of new touchpoints. These principles, ideally, should be inspirational and descriptive, rather than hard-and-fast rules. They are intended to inspire creativity, not to take the place of designers and engineers (and their expertise). As a friend of ours, Davis Masten, once put it, they should "facilitate designers' intuition."

For example, in the discussion of opportunity spaces, you saw that PC makers have a major opportunity when people set up a new tablet. What they want is excitement and ease—maybe even wonder— but what they get is often discomfort, frustration, and anger. The difference between what's wanted and what's being delivered is huge.

The design principles could be as simple as the following:

- Develop every touchpoint to excite people or trigger wonder.
- Show the possibilities of the offering to enhance interest.
- Design to communicate ease of setup.
- Minimize setup steps.
- Show how each setup step enhances the sense of possibility overall.
- Don't require the user to do anything the tablet can do itself.

In other words, the purpose is to guide, not determine. Ideally, such principles should both inspire and act as yardsticks against which any new touchpoint concept could be measured.

Reframing

Several years ago, a group of Nathan's students entered the Rotman Business Plan competition in Toronto, Canada. That year, it was sponsored by one of the largest banks in the world, which challenged students to find a way for it to connect more effectively with college students. Unfortunately, Nathan's students discovered from their research that college students were on to banks (meaning: they didn't trust or like them). They were smart enough to know that the offers of free checks and credit cards with punitive terms weren't great deals. They saw these tactics as predatory behavior that ensnared them into an endless cycle of debt, credit overdrafts, and interest. They disliked whenever one of these offers came in the mail or was handed out on campus because it was just another reminder of how greedy and impersonal they viewed banks.

These students wanted better relationships with financial institutions—but big banks had, unfortunately, burned these bridges. Large institutions were dead to them. Nathan's students then told the bank that it was going to be a waste of time and money to try new messaging or a new gimmick to get these kids on board. Such an approach wouldn't go over well, and the odds of success were slim.

Sometimes, however, discovering uncovers additional possibilities that can present bigger opportunities. In this case, Nathan's students learned that while with students as a whole, the bank had no chance, foreign students were a different matter altogether. It was impossible for them to get government-backed, low-interest student loans in the United States and Canada, and the ones they could obtain in their home countries had exorbitant rates. If the bank could assess the risk more effectively (the team devised a way to do this), it could serve these students and create an entirely new business model with a multibillion-dollar opportunity.

In other words, they had reframed the challenge. Their research led them away from the initial question and toward an entirely different insight. This can often happen at the end of discovering, and it's critically important to make sure that you don't miss any of the opportunities it reveals. Often, the phase reveals that the initial goals can't be realized or aren't as advantageous as initially assumed and that you need to reframe around better opportunities.

Of course, it's never easy to go back to your clients or managers and tell them that the opportunity they've assumed—the one for which they've even budgeted time, money, and resources—simply isn't a good one. In the case of Nathan's students, the bank gave them a polite thank you and selected a different team that presented a more traditional approach—an app! As his students predicted, they didn't yield significant gains in either relationship or business.

If innovation is your aim, you can't ignore the opportunity to reframe. And you have to be ready to pivot.

EYE OPENERS

This chapter does a deep dive into the research phase of relationship innovation. Called *discovering*, it involves deploying specific techniques to uncover what your customers are getting from your relationship with them, and what they really want. Then it's important to construct current and desired wavelines, as well as document the core meanings, pace, and triggers to help your innovation team understand how to improve relationships. Reframing then logically follows. Some questions to get you thinking are:

- In what way do you overvalue quantitative insights?

- What human factors are biasing your quantitative data collection?

- How could you sell qualitative research internally?

- What could you do if you understood what your customers truly valued in their lives? Would it make a difference?

- What does your current product, service, and packaging look, sound, feel, and smell like? Does it trigger the right responses in your customers?

- How do your customers experience change? Will it be difficult to innovate on their time frame?

8

Deciding

Now that you have defined where your opportunities lie, you might think the next step is to scope out and ramp up a design team. Not so fast. Because relationship innovation is a strategic process that can affect your entire business, you have a few extra steps before moving forward.

First, decide what to do. Obviously, you can't attack every opportunity space you have uncovered. Instead, look at practical considerations, such as cost versus benefit. But, more importantly, you also have to consider whether the innovation direction is right for your customers, your brand, and even your own people. And you have to make sure that everyone in your organization knows where you're headed in relationship terms. You can't *become* by doing unless you know what you're trying to become.

This chapter talks about a key phase of the innovation process: deciding. Essentially, you have to understand the impact of your proposed innovations on your business in a holistic way. Then you need to prepare everyone for change. That way, you won't innovate in a vacuum, and as so often happens, come up with great ideas and products that blindside your organization and fail because you're not ready.

Ready for Change

After the discovering phase, you understand what your customers want and the opportunity spaces where you can innovate. But before you start, you need to make sure you have something else: an organization that's ready for change. To show how it can go wrong, let's start with a story about a project that uncovered a great innovation opportunity and why the organization failed to capitalize on it.

A few years ago, Steve was hired by the innovation and research group at a large health insurance provider. They wanted to find out what their customers really wanted and the experiences they'd like to have. Steve helped them through the discovering phase and presented them with his team's findings.

In their work, they had learned that the central experiences of people entering the company's system were a lack of control and a lack of connection. They did not feel they were talking with real people, nor did they have any sense that they had a choice in what they were doing. Instead, they were interacting with a large bureaucracy whose processes they didn't understand and whose services and benefits were largely opaque. Naturally, that produced fear and anxiety, especially because many of the people who signed up with this particular healthcare provider only did so because they had no other choice. They had a dependency on the company, not a two-way relationship. Not surprisingly, most said they would quickly change providers if they could find another viable alternative. This was a big problem.

Steve's team made what seems like a sensible recommendation. They suggested that the company change its approach. It should innovate to make the entry process more transparent and more convenient for customers. It should also make them feel like they were in control and driving the interaction. This was an achievable goal. Many hospitals have doctors and nurses who focus on educating patients and ensuring they understand their choices. The organization simply needed to commit to change.

Unfortunately, the company did not accept the findings. The idea was too foreign to its managers, who were a financially focused bunch. They designed their services based on actuarial data. Wherever they could save dollars, they did. And they had little inclination to spend more for a benefit that they couldn't easily grasp. For example, they did not want their doctors to spend more time with patients—they wanted them to see more patients each day and bill more for services. The idea that their doctors could have a sense of freedom and control was scary to them. It had implications they didn't want to consider. It would force them to recognize that costs weren't the only thing driving value in the healthcare ecosystem.

Steve also had the wrong client inside the organization. He was working with an innovation group that declined to make the recommendations to management. The changes would have been so sweeping, the group reasoned, that they lay outside their authority to suggest. Though they knew that these ideas could result in better health care, the team presumed that their leaders wouldn't be interested in value that wasn't rooted in actuarial-table evaluations of opportunities. Good ideas died as a result.

This is an important lesson. Relationship innovation often involves broad changes in approach that cut across entire organizations. That's why the decision process needs to involve the highest levels of management, which can push to drive change. It also means that an organization has to be capable of change and prepared for it. That's what deciding is all about.

The first step in deciding is to review the opportunities identified in your research. These will have been illustrated in the waveline diagram if you've followed our template and examples. For each one, you need to decide which ones are the best opportunities for your organization and come up with a rough idea of what you could do to improve the experience and the business. Typically, we advise not starting with a proposed solution, but thinking in more abstract terms:

1. First, look at the experiential outcome you want to create for your customer. You can find this in your waveline diagram. Typically, it consists of a single experience, such as wonder, oneness, excitement. This should be the focus of your thinking on what to build.

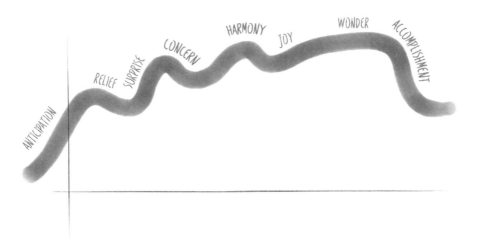

2. Next, decide abstractly what kind of touchpoints would work best to achieve this. Start by determining whether you want to have a top-down, co-created, or improvisational relationship with customers. (See Chapter 2, "Defining a Business Relationship," for more on this topic.)

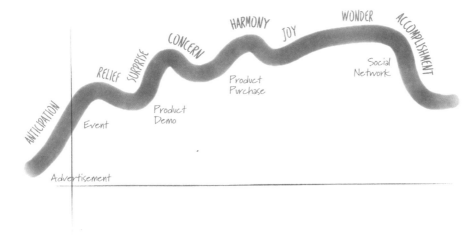

3. Then develop rough tactics that would achieve the outcome. These need not be full concepts, but a rough idea of the capabilities that will be needed to achieve them.

4. Don't be afraid to step outside your comfort zones. Your company may be good at certain things. It may have no experience with improvisational interaction. That's fine. At this point, you're simply trying to decide what kinds of things you should do.

The final point is to leave plenty of freedom for designers to shape the touchpoints as they like. Nothing you do should be prescriptive. In this phase, you're not coming up with the full solution; rather, you're trying to look at your options and decide where to concentrate your efforts.

Decisions, Decisions

At this point, it's time to decide which of the proposed directions it makes the most sense to pursue. The first step, obviously, is to weigh cost and benefit. Clearly, you don't want to build anything that won't help you achieve your customers' desired experience and relationship.

But more importantly, you need to know if it will be right for your customers and doable for your organization as a whole.

To do this, you need to answer a few questions:

- How can you build the options?

- Which can you sustain?

- Which options can provide the greatest ROI?

- Which customers are willing to pay for the new experiences—current or new?

- How will they connect with your brand promise?

- How much disruption will it cause to your business?

Let's take a look at these in detail.

Building and Sustaining

The first decision you need to make is whether you can actually build and, more importantly, sustain new relationships. For example, imagine you run a national chain of health and beauty spas. From your discovering phase, you realize that your customers get a great sense of beauty and self-worth from your services, but that the effect wears off in a few days. Then they fall back into feeling ordinary again. You believe that you could continue to provide meaning in their lives by offering them helpful tips between visits, so they can feel better about themselves on an ongoing basis.

One way you could do that is to build an app and encourage clients to download it. The app could ping them with tips, advice, and also offers. But, as a beauty company, you know you can't build it yourself. That's not part of your core competency or that of your IT team. However, you do hire outside agencies to help you with web and mobile design, so you can ask one to build it for you. You also set up an internal team to provision it with content.

But you also know something else. Apps have to change with the times. As a spa, you need to make sure that the interface keeps pace with other beauty apps, both in terms of what it offers as well as how it looks. Styles and times change, and you can't ever look boring or old-fashioned. In other words, you and your partners need to come up with a plan to keep it up-to-date.

Building and sustaining are core features of any innovation. Anyone can come up with a brilliant idea, but you have to look beyond it and think what it will cost to keep it going.

Promising the Highest Return on Investment

Clearly, if you have several opportunity spaces and promising new concepts for each, it's vital that you evaluate the potential value (financial and otherwise) of each option. The "normal" financial metrics are very much relevant here, from costs such as development, raw materials, retooling, sales, promotion, and so on, as well as the attention any new innovation requires from management. Customer-centered innovation doesn't replace these types of calculations. It simply ups the prospect of developing concepts more likely to do well with those customers.

Getting Your Customers Ready

Any good discovery process uncovers the kinds of experiences your customers want. But will they pay for them? And if they will, will they pay enough to make it worthwhile? Your customers may say they want their dishwasher to send them a text message when the cycle is complete. But it makes a huge difference if that capability will add $1 or $150 to the cost. You have to make sure that the relationship will not come at a cost that encourages them to buy elsewhere.

Defining Brand Appropriateness

Any innovation in relationship will have an impact on brands in three possible ways. It can be perfectly within customer expectations as well as the goals of your brand. This presents no problem. Also, it can be a stretch but doable. Your customers may want a particular set of experiences, but they may not see you as the right company for them—until you can demonstrate otherwise. That requires additional investment to get them to accept this change and see you in a new light.

The final possibility is that an innovation can also be completely out of brand alignment, in which case you should avoid it. For example, Microsoft has been successful selling technological solutions to businesses of all sizes, but it's shown no affinity with or ability to understand fashion. Whereas it might be possible to build wearable devices, it's unlikely that it could successfully move into core fashion, like evening dresses.

Working for the Business

Sometimes, people want things that are outside your business's capacity to provide—and not necessarily what you want to do. McDonald's and Wendy's may have customers who would like to have the added convenience of someone taking their order tableside, but that's not going to work, given the efficiencies of the organizations. Of course, in considering this question, you have to realize that there will always be resistance to change, and you need to weed out what's truly impossible from what your people simply don't feel like doing.

Setting Pace and Intensity

In addition to deciding which opportunities to pursue, you also have to understand the pace and intensity needed in order to please the target market. Luckily, your discovery phase has also let you in on your customers' preferred pace of change.

Typically, the pace of change will vary depending on the kind of experiences your customers would like to have. For example, imagine that your solutions are based on evoking a sense of oneness with your company. And that your work with customers has suggested that the pace of change will require that your service be adjusted once every three months. In contrast, if you focus on wonder, the service might have to evolve every week. Based on this understanding, you have some decisions to make about how you want to proceed.

EYE OPENERS

This chapter looked at *deciding.* To do so, you select the best opportunity spaces for success and then evaluate them on your ability to deliver, as well as whether they are right for your customers, your organization, and, of course, if they are lucrative enough to justify the capital investment.

Use the following questions to start thinking about deciding:

- In what way is your company culturally aligned for relationship innovation?

- How is your management committed to innovation?

- What are some of the cultural considerations you have that might resist innovation?

- What kinds of innovation might be too much for your customers? What might they welcome?

9

Declaring

This chapter looks at the important step of declaring your intentions within the organization (or within your client's), recognizing that it's not as simple as making a statement. Instead, it's about setting the stage for becoming a different kind of organization as well.

After you make decisions about what you want to do, you now need to prepare your organization for disruptive change. Do that now with a step called *declaring.* In essence, it refers to informing a company about the new strategies and making a declaration that promises a new relationship with customers. To do this, create and deliver a message that educates those in charge of creating, supporting, and managing those promises. This might be a document or an event or a combination of several internal touchpoints. You then use your innovation team's members to evangelize your intentions. The point of this step is part fair warning (people are more able to deal with change when they know it's coming) and part garnering buy-in (the essence of leadership is communicating a clear vision of the future that others *want* to follow—and this is your chance to present that vision).

A Relationship Statement and Brand Positioning

With relationship innovation, you're often signaling a shift in how you act and communicate. Sometimes, this requires you to rethink your brand, starting with your brand's position. Articulating what kind of relationship you want to develop with your customer in a "relationship statement" is an effective way to maintain clarity with the organization about your relationship goals. The statement can be very simple, stating the type of relationship you're going to focus on—top-down, co-created, and so on—and the types of experiences you seek to evoke for customers. Once you do this, you're in a great position to construct a brand positioning that embodies your relationship goals.

Just to review, the purpose of a brand positioning is to articulate clearly what a company intends to stand for with its customers and its employees. The value of such a positioning is that, when properly constructed, it unifies corporate goals and target market needs in a simple, easy-to-follow manner. Ultimately, it can serve as the yardstick against which new offerings are measured. In short, it is the essence of strategy.

Brand positionings are constructed in any number of ways. Although there's no one, right way to describe a brand positioning, it's essential that it be very easy to use. People with the responsibility of developing any sort of messaging and communications, as well as new products and services, should be inspired and guided by it, so their work consistently reinforces its central ideas. Similar to a relationship statement, putting a brand positioning in the form of a statement provides useful guidance to everyone in a company.

The typical brand positioning statement contains four components, as follows:

- **The customer.** This is the person you seek to serve.

- **The promise.** This is a global statement of the mission of the company, product, or service. It often leans toward what management sees as the core reason the company is in business, from the point of view of customer needs and desires (as opposed to simply stockholder or employee interests).

- **The benefits.** Often, these are higher-level and emotional or meaning-oriented, such as accomplishment, transcendence, beauty, and so on.

- **The features.** These exist within products and services that, from the customer point of view, deliver the desired benefits. These might not necessarily be what the company automatically thinks of as the key features.

A template of a positioning statement might look like the following.[1]

_____ **(Company X)** exists to
provide _____ **(customer)** with
_____ **(a key promise)**. In so doing,
it delivers _____, _____,
and _____ **(benefits)** to customers.
Toward that end, it offers _____,
_____, and _____
**(features the market believes produces
the benefits)**.

1. There is an inherent problem with these templates in that they're often used lazily. Sometimes, strategists simply fill in each blank with what they think is right in a process that most closely resembles the zany game "Mad Libs." To be used correctly, each blank should be filled in and supported from the insights gained from discovery to ensure not only that the statement is accurate but also that it reflects the priorities that drive customer decisions.

How does this look in practice? The next figure shows a fully made-up example for Disney that can shed light on how to do this.

> **Disney (Company X)** exists to provide **families worldwide (the customer)** with **wholesome, uplifting entertainment (the promise)**. In so doing, it provides **entertainment, fun, and family togetherness (higher-level benefits)** to customers. Toward that end, it offers **feature films, theme parks, and subdivisions (the features)**.

A relationship statement looks pretty much the same, overall. The only real differences are that the promise is specifically designed to describe the kind of relationship you're going to have with customers and the benefits are explicitly experiential in nature. But these differences make for huge implications when declaring your intent, as follows:

> **Disney (Company X)** exists to provide **families worldwide (the customer)** with **ever-deepening wonder (the promise)**. In so doing, it provides **solace, beauty, community, and validation of core values (higher-level benefits)** to customers. Toward that end, it offers **feature films, theme parks, and subdivisions (the features)**.

The difference is immediately obvious. The latter sets your direction out in a way that is more engaging, must develop over time, and is all about how customers are changed by interacting with the company's touchpoints. When a relationship statement is declared, employees can understand the full objectives of innovation efforts, as well as how daunting it can be to get there. For companies that are already culturally inclined to risk-taking, it can be an exhilarating declaration.

To emphasize the excitement rather than the fear, the statement should be accompanied by:

1. A waveline diagram for each segment.

2. An explanation of the current relationships you offer and their shortcomings.

3. An explanation of the relationships you want to have with customers (and why).

4. An overview of the decisions you've made for innovation to evoke the right experiences for your customers.

5. A how-to for employees (and, possibly, partners) so that they can support your company moving forward.

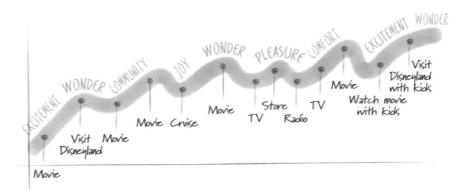

For example, imagine you're a sports brand. The discovering phase uncovered that although your customers buy your products frequently, they want to have closer, more frequent contact with your company. They want a greater feeling of community; for example, they want to feel like you're a partner in accomplishing their goals.

The broader statement would first explain why that's not happening today. For example, you might be too promotion-focused, or trying too hard to drive sales, rather than building relationships. The statement would then explain how you plan to improve your relationships. Your tactics might include in-store clinics, a fitness app, sponsoring youth teams, or any number of things. The statement would then describe what decisions you've made and where you're heading. Finally, it would show how staff should behave whenever they're acting as representatives of your company. In this case, the statement might focus on listening, giving positive encouragement, and even empathizing with a customer's experience by telling a story.

In other words, this document provides an organizational and also personal roadmap for employees to understand their place in delivering the evolving relationship.

Evangelizing

The relationship statement is also a critical tool that your innovation team can use to evangelize the new relationships. By "evangelizing," we mean that you need to proactively advance discussions all around the organization about building valued customer relationships. Even though you don't know exactly what you're going to build at this point (because you haven't actually designed solutions), you do have a good idea of what you're going to become for your customers.

That said, merely talking or distributing a document isn't enough. In addition to sending it around, you also advocate for more experiential ways of reaching an audience. Some ideas include the following:

- **Role-playing.** It's hard to act a new way without practice. That's why it's usually a good idea to conduct exercises in which people try out the new company relationships. Your innovation team evangelists can observe and instruct their fellow employees on getting it right.

- **Designed spaces.** You can design events and spaces to help people understand what they're supposed to do. For example, when Steve was at the market insights firm Cheskin, his team once prepared an entire floor of exhibits for clothes buyers so that Levi's employees could understand what customers wanted. These exhibits were physical incarnations of the firm's research and even featured real customers who had brought in substantial parts of their wardrobes from home. Having customers on hand enabled employees to ask directly how they mixed and matched clothes, what they wore in different settings and to different events, and how they perceived their needs in different contexts.

- **Videos.** Typically, your research includes plenty of videos that explain what customers want. With careful editing, you can drive home what the desired experiences are and how your company might deliver them. This works especially well for larger organizations, where it's not easy to evangelize to everyone individually.

- **Interactive support.** Some people learn best on their own. For them, you can also design interactive teaching tools that help make real the kinds of experiences you're trying to evoke.

Whatever you do, however, it's important to make sure that everyone understands what's expected of them and where the organization is headed. The earlier you do this, the better, because it often takes time to put a new face on things.

EYE OPENERS

This chapter focused on an underappreciated phase of relationship innovation: declaring. You learned about the relationship statement that explains where you are now, where you hope to be, what decisions you've made to help you get there, and, ultimately, who you hope to be for your customers. That way, you can get everyone started in the process and align them to your roadmap for better customer experiences in the future.

You can use the following questions to start thinking about declaring:

- What would be the best way, in your context, to evangelize for a new vision of the relationship you want to have with your customers?

- How do new relationships enhance the organization's strategies (and vice versa)?

10

Designing

At this point in your journey, it's time to start making touchpoints. Let's face it—this can be a little scary. All of the work you've done so far has been preparation for that big blank sheet of paper (or nowadays, more likely, a screen) that you'll use to create ideas and concepts, and develop them into something new. Needless to say, many find this a disorienting and difficult moment. Many businesspeople treat this phase as just another check box on the to-do list.

It's not.

Designing the offering is the most complex phase, the most critical, and although incredibly ambiguous and anxiety-producing for those who feel safe with a set recipe, the most fun.

However, this phase is often fraught with perils: everyone has an opinion on every detail. Whether they have professional experience to offer or not, most can't see the finish line until it's upon them (or even past them, in some cases), many aren't patient enough to deal with the inevitable ambiguity required for the design process, and most can't suspend their disbelief in order for new, better solutions to arise.

This phase can also be the most contentious because (finally) there will be tangible solutions to judge. Until now, the research, reports, and decisions were real but abstract. Now, they become concrete, and everyone will have an opinion, now that they can see results that may or may not match their expectations. In a real sense, this process is its own waveline, a story of the development journey your peers and superiors go through in visualizing and accepting new solutions that represent a new way of approaching business. It is not without its own trials, and it can just as certainly be designed to flow better or worse.

Luckily, you've laid a good foundation. Your research has revealed who your customers are and what they really want and need. You've prepared your organization for new solutions and framed your approach to build relationships and premium value. And you know the outcomes you seek. As a result, you have a great roadmap for making touch-points—a roadmap for design.

That said, design is easily the most critical, creative, and unfortunately ambiguous phase of relationship innovation. This chapter looks at the tools and requirements for great design and offers a rough process for moving forward. The one thing this book can't do? Make magic happen. That has to come from you.

Designing Is a Team Sport

Throughout your first few phases of becoming by doing (explained in Chapter 5, "Becoming by Doing"), you've relied on a large innovation team. You've had representatives from all impacted parts of the company—including marketing, PR, and customer service—on board. Now it's time to break off the core group of people who will actually create the new and improved touchpoints for your company.

Designing always takes a team. Even though you may hear about lone inventors, they really don't exist anymore—and maybe never have. Developing all but the most simple of products and services requires multiple skills and expertise that you rarely find in one person. Instead, you bring together a talented group with expertise in the relevant areas of creating a product or service, including, at the very least, designers and engineers.

With multiple disciplines working together, a design team also needs a strong leader who can keep all of those skills, egos, and perspectives together. This person, of course, need not be the best designer, but rather someone who is able to keep everyone on track with the same understanding of priorities and possibilities. Often, this person is the one with the most compelling vision for the solution.

The team leader needs to be able to make tough, practical decisions while maintaining an atmosphere of respect, openness, and adherence to the vision; the ability to listen is critical. The best ideas could come from anyone, regardless of whether that person fully understands the technical or financial implications of the solution. A team member may have fresh perspectives that lead to important ideas about the design, even though creative thinking may not be his or her strength or focus. Whatever the case, the leader must keep those ideas developing. The team has to keep flowing, decision to decision, and making progress, or you may need to reassess your leadership.

IDEAS CAN COME FROM ANYWHERE

Whenever discussing where ideas can come from, we like to talk about
a bridge, whose builders found their inspiration in an unlikely source:
a sewing machine.

That bridge is known as the Millau Viaduct, and it solves a massive traffic
problem by passing a chokepoint in the north/south traffic between Spain
and France. For years, every car and truck on the route had to pass through
a small, medieval town called Millau. Settled more than 3,000 years ago,
it is situated in a deep valley, the Tarn, where two rivers join together.
The town boasts a 12th century belfry and nearby caves where Roquefort
cheese is made. Needless to say, it wasn't designed for the needs of modern transportation. In particular, during the vacation month of August, it
became clogged with traffic jams.

It was obvious to everyone that a bypass was needed, but that posed a big
problem. The Tarn Valley was quite deep and featured strong winds—
both of which made construction of a bridge difficult and dangerous.
Nonetheless, in 1991, the French government began design work on what
would eventually become the world's tallest bridge, rising 1,125 feet above
the valley floor.

NIGEL YOUNG/FOSTER + PARTNERS

Building the supports for the bridge was a difficult but solvable problem using traditional construction methods. Laying the road bed was another matter altogether. Not only was it at a considerable elevation, but the winds also made the work hazardous. As a result, traditional construction techniques were either too costly or too risky to consider.

Luckily, the overall project leader Marc Buonomo had once worked in a very different context: a clothing factory. Thinking about the problem, he realized that laying the steel deck of a bridge might not be all that different from how you stitch together the legs on a pair of pants. Rather than building in place, you could build it on one end, and slide it across the supports, much like a piece of cloth being fed into a sewing machine. He enlisted the help of American multinational Enerpac to get the job done. Essentially, they built the world's largest spool feed, complete with hydraulic lifts that gently lifted and placed the road bed onto the supports as it was eased across them. Amazingly enough, the solution worked, and the project was completed both on time and for far less money than anticipated.

The key, of course, was that Buonomo was able to bring a completely different point of view to the problem at hand. Almost no one who works in construction knows about industrial sewing machines, but the principles from one field applied to another, translated through his experience and perception. Put simply, you can find inspiration anywhere and everywhere—even in the most unlikely places.

The Design Process

When it comes to a design process, you have many to choose from. The good news is that although they differ in some ways, most share fundamental similarities, and almost all can work well with the relationship insights described in this book. Instead of going through these processes in detail, we will simply outline the major elements of a good process and encourage you to find more detailed descriptions elsewhere.

Generally speaking, design consists of four activities: concept generation, prototyping, testing, and iteration.[1] You have many options for accomplishing each one, but overall they are relatively simple to understand.

Concept Generation

This is exactly what it sounds like. The discovering phase has uncovered challenges and opportunities to improve your customers' experience of your company. Now you have to generate new ways to solve those challenges using either structured exercises, like brainstorming, or unstructured processes that rely more on designers' intuition.

If you're looking for ways to come up with new ideas, there's a great free resource called the Human Centered Design Toolkit. It was developed by IDEO for the Bill & Melinda Gates Foundation and can be found online at www.ideo.com/work/human-centered-design-toolkit. Although it was intended to help nongovernmental organizations (NGOs) devise innovative solutions to the world's problems, it provides a wealth of information and techniques for devising new ideas. These techniques can work for any business or organization.

---

1. Note: Most books on the design process also include preparation and research phases that are similar to the Discovering phase. Because of the holistic nature of relationship innovation and its impact on entire organizations, use a more inclusive team for the research and decision phases than is common.

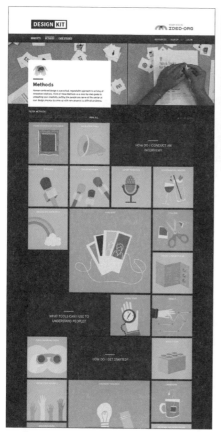

Of course, sometimes design teams get stuck and are unable to come up with anything. In that case, move away from what's not working. Instead, switch up your ideation process and try a new tool.

Prototyping

When you generate your ideas, it's time to start building a solution. Designers often call this phase *thinking by doing*. In other words, you're not entirely certain what the eventual solution will be, but simply by working on it and building things, you often discover new and better ways to get the job done. That's why you should begin building a prototype (or a preliminary model) as soon as you can. You can talk, analyze, and strategize all day, but you'll never actually make something until you start to build.

Building an initial prototype is the scariest part of the innovation process. It's not uncommon to face a blank screen, piece of paper, or lump of clay and wonder if you'll ever be able to make something wonderful out of it.

First, note that it's okay to be scared. Even designers with fantastic track records often feel pangs of doubt at this moment. You can reduce the fear by having low expectations of the initial prototype. You can purposely create rough builds of ideas so that you can start solving problems rather than trying to create beautiful end solutions. You can always improve a prototype as you go along, and it's immensely easier to perfect an existing thing than it is to build something perfect from scratch. This is the real secret of design: you begin by making *something*—anything really—that you know will need to be improved over time. Then you work to improve it.

Of course, like much of what we suggest in this book, prototyping is not always an easy thing to pitch to a business. To many managers, it may look like busywork or wasted time. Or they may not understand the purpose of an early prototype; they may want to cancel the project and jettison the team because they don't like what they see. The truth is that design is a messy process, and designers typically hide the chaos to ensure autonomy while working. A business may believe it is paying for a single logo, when, in fact, it's paying for dozens of prototype logos that are tested and don't work as well as one that does.

Unfortunately, becoming by doing doesn't always make it easy to hide the prototype. Ideally, you have contact with a larger team that's plugged into the organization. It's best if everyone understands the need to play around with ideas up front and has their expectations appropriately set for the process, the timeline, and the nature of each deliverable along the way. Your team needs space to experiment—sometimes wildly. In enterprises, finding this space can be the riskiest and most critical part of the design process.

Testing

After you have a prototype that feels like it's going somewhere, you should test it. In most situations, we advise small tests, conducted in informal settings. This not only saves money, but it also helps you learn how successful your designs are in producing the right experiences for customers. You can't test everything at once, of course—especially with early prototypes that are minimally functional. And you can't wait to test until the prototype represents all of the functions, either. Start with important, major features, test those, and then move on to other ones. You can fold together these prototypes along the way, but don't try to build—and test—everything at once.

What do you look for in your tests? Traditionally, designers have always tested functions like usability and whether their audience wants the product. You still need to test those things, but you should also look at the concepts we've been talking about in this book: how emotions and meanings rise, fall, and evolve over time; whether the rhythm of change is right for customers; and how you've adequately (or wonderfully) transitioned them into and out of the experiences you've built for them. You also need to test whether your customers understand the value of what you've designed for them. You need to know whether you've actually made their lives easier, improved their experiences, shifted their emotions, and engaged them on a deeper level. You need to test the choices that trigger responses in your customers so that they react to the design with the kind of impact you envision. If you merely assess whether you've met their functional needs, you'll miss the whole point of the premium value and relationship you're trying to develop.

However, testing does require some investment, and you may wonder whether you should skip it or reduce it to a minimum so that you can concentrate on creation. This is a mistake. Testing brings a number of important advantages to any innovation effort:

- **It checks assumptions.** No matter how much you distance yourself and accept the results of discovery, design still involves making many decisions about what will evoke the experiences and relationships your customers want. The only way to be sure you're right is by testing those decisions with customers.

- **It saves money overall.** The earlier you find a problem, the less expensive it is to fix. It's better to find out early if your form factor is puzzling in a Chinese context, or if an interface concept is too complicated. You also want to know if what you're creating is tedious and frustrating, even though your intentions were otherwise.

- **It uncovers solutions.** Tests not only reveal problems, but sometimes they actually point to touchpoints working better than you think. That can provide important insight that drives further decisions down the line.

Simply put, testing is something you should do early and often.

A final point about user testing is that sometimes it will result in failure. It will tell you that your users don't like what you've created. In that case, you have to be honest and not try to rationalize away the results of a test. If something doesn't work, it doesn't work. Nathan once met with engineers at a large software firm to discuss the latest version of their product. As he detailed its shortcomings, one of them got exasperated and said, "You just don't understand the user model!" Nathan replied, "I'm the user. It's my model."

If a test fails, don't get frustrated. Instead, go back to your waveline diagrams and personas and remind yourself who you were designing for in the first place.

Iteration

In the iteration phase, you go back to your prototype, respond to the results of your testing, and make improvements. Then test again, improve, and so on until you reach a working solution.

On the surface, iteration is a fairly straightforward process, but there are a few considerations to keep in mind. For complex solutions, do not rely on a single prototype. There are many simultaneous prototypes for different parts of the experience in different media and channels. In that case, as is probably obvious, you should test parts of the solution when they're ready and combine them as they near completion.

Also, the iteration phase can extend past your ship date. You should look at a released product as simply another prototype. You can see how it does in the marketplace, get feedback from users, and iterate again with a newer version. In this sense, you never stop iterating— a fact that can sometimes free you from seeking perfection that never comes (and a product that, therefore, never ships).

SERVICES AND DESIGN

Services offer a special case for prototyping. Because they are always on, they can constantly and continuously evolve. You may not even be able to replace a service with a new version—or your customers may not want one. Instead, you can tweak and improve your offerings based on their performance and needs. After all, there is no perfect design and no perfect answer to a customer's concerns. Solutions must be continuously upgraded, as much as you can.

The MVP Problem

It's become popular these days, especially with digital solutions, to see a start-up release, sometimes called a *minimum viable product*, or MVP. The idea is that you scrape together something that has the most important functionality of a service—and often little else. Such offerings are acknowledged to be incomplete, but are understood to have enough functionality to get the job done and into the market ASAP. A start-up's investment may be tied to releasing the MVP, which is, in turn, usually limited by the amount of funds and time available. The team then continues to add more features as they have time and resources, and hopefully, watch customer use to improve the product.

The idea of an MVP is a good one (it's usually not possible to build-out everything you intend from the start), but it's a very misunderstood concept and has a significant drawback for relationship innovation: it only works if you intend to deliver functional value. This is the biggest blind spot in the technology industry. Thousands of start-ups in Silicon Valley (and more all over the world) die not because what they produced was poorly made but because of two reasons: it didn't really do anything that anyone outside of the development needed or wanted, and it didn't compare to the total experience customers could get from competing offerings. By trying to keep teams and companies focused (a good thing), MVPs more often keep them focused only on functional value.

A better way to think about this (and label it) is MVE: minimal viable experience. Or, maybe MVR: minimal viable relationship (since that's really what you're trying to build). In these terms, function is only part of what's delivered and often not the most important part. There's a famous diagram circling the start-up world now that illustrates this point.

Minimum Viable Product

Emotional design
Usable
Reliable
Functional

Not this

This

Emotional design
Usable
Reliable
Functional

@jopas

September 2014 | With compliments to Aaron Walter

Microsoft created an MVP when it launched the Zune (a failed competitor to the iPod), but it paled in comparison to the experience and relationship available from Apple's iPod at the time. It was actually a worthy rival to the iPod itself, but that's not all there was to the relationship. The iPod, combined with iTunes, the iTunes Store, audiobooks, videos, and many other services created an entire ecosystem around the iPod that offered a much more enhanced relationship. It was a world of delight, not just a product. What Microsoft had to do to compete was to offer at least as good an experience to build a relationship upon, if not a better one.

The same is true of most start-ups. Delivering functionality at a comparable price won't create lasting, valuable customer relationships. If they already have experiences with competitors that are richer, more engaging, and more valuable relationships, you must up your game dramatically. Of course, for a start-up, it's often not possible to fully compete with what already exists. But merely offering more function, instead of value on more premium levels, can't be successful because it engages people in shallower, not deeper, ways.

We can explain this by using a movie as an analogy. Movies, done right, produce an experiential journey with their viewers. But imagine if you screened a prototype of an action movie that had all of the strictly necessary plot components, but left out all of the character development scenes. You'd know what happened, but you wouldn't care about the people it happened to. You wouldn't have a series of experiences with it; you'd merely be looking at a dry, uninteresting recounting of events.

You can't fake premium value. You can't fake a relationship. If you want to build one, you have to engage your customers' emotions, values, identity, and core meanings. Most people don't live in an MVP world and don't want minimum value products, so an MVP isn't going to satisfy them. Your customers want to be provided with product functionality, but they also want to be engaged in more valuable ways. If you hope to compete with Apple, you can't expect to win by having a more feature-rich product or a lower price. That's not the game Apple is playing. Instead, it offers a rich, complex set of offerings that engage people on multiple, deep levels.

In other words, if you set your design sights too low or frame the challenge in terms that are too narrow, you'll miss the mark by a mile. Many innovators have this blind spot. Although they have every reason to focus, minimize risk, and get to market quickly, getting there with too little never works. You don't need to have the first solution in the market; you need to have the right one.

Design as Curation

Design is not synonymous with originality. To succeed, you don't need to be wildly unique, create entirely new products, or set bold new trends. Sometimes this happens, but more often, a good designer builds things that reflect trends and incorporate elements already established by the culture.

That's why a thorough understanding of your customer's reactions to various design elements is so important. You uncover not only the relationships people want, but also the triggers—such as colors, materials, flavors, aromas, typography, and imagery—that would affect them in the way they want. Use those triggers as design elements to evoke the feelings and experiences you want your customers to have.

Their choices, of course, aren't necessarily the ones you'd make for yourself. If you're a visually sophisticated designer creating a watch for yourself, you'd probably make very different choices about form, color, and materials than your customers would. A bamboo watch may seem cool, new, and eco-conscious to you, but it may trigger entirely different reactions in people who lack your aesthetic sensibilities. In that case, you need to put aside those personal preferences and stick to what discovering tells you. Ultimately, design is not about what managers, designers, or developers like, it's about how every decision creates and reinforces the experiences that you know will be successful with your customers.

Designers need to be curators of these triggers. You can't rely on your customers to tell you what to do because they almost never know the possibilities or have a vision for enhanced solutions. But you aren't designing for statistics either. You're also not designing for yourself. It makes the process more challenging, but you need to make design choices that reflect how your customers react and what they understand. Doing this well and still being original is what separates the best designers.

Data and Design

The designer-as-curator approach doesn't reduce design simply to the process of parroting back research findings. Designers still need to use their considerable experience, preferences, and inspiration to make decisions about triggers and integrate them into a meaningful, pleasing whole for others. Data and research only get you so far before intuition has to take over.

This point was amusingly proved by the artists Komar and Melamid in a fascinating project called *Paint by Numbers*. In it, they polled ordinary people in several countries about what they felt great art was. The polls were quite scientific, using over 100 questions and a rigorous statistical methodology. When the data came back, the artists analyzed it and came to two major conclusions. First, everyone hated contemporary art. Second, they all thought they wanted blue landscapes, green fields, overhanging trees, and a nice expanse of seawater.

Based on this data, they then created most-wanted paintings for the countries. If a certain preference was strong, such as wanting cows in the field before the water, cows it would be. If everyone wanted a deciduous tree with summer foliage, in one went. In the end, the paintings for the different countries looked surprisingly similar: landscapes with an expanse of ultra-green grass to the left, usually with a promontory overlooking a stretch of water to the right.

The two artists then toured the respective countries with these paintings and asked people for their reactions. The result? Nobody liked them very much. Neither critics nor rural grandmothers. The art didn't work at all. The data was right, but the solution it suggested, without interpretation, was clichéd and boring.

Another example from the commercial world is the now-infamous story about Google testing 41 different shades of blue to determine the best one for the color of a button. The problem is that this is too reductive. Design challenges are much more complicated. If you test colors for a corporate logo, you may find one that the vast majority of people like. But that color may also be too close to one of your competitors, which would make it impossible for you to stand out.

The one point you can take away from this is to not follow data and research slavishly. Merely because you've gathered a lot of information does not mean you can't deviate from it. Rather, any good solution is going to require significant creative interpretation.

The creative people at YouTube capture the idea perfectly when they talk about data *informing* design, not *prescribing* it. You want to make sure anything you make reflects qualitative and quantitative research in the discovering phase, but you still need to leave the field open for how you get there.

Design and Variable Time

In most customer relationships, the time it takes individual customers to react to your products and services can vary greatly. If your dentist tells you that you have a cavity, you'll go through roughly the same sequence of events as anyone else in a similar situation. But the spaces between the steps could be longer or shorter than those of another person. You could have the cavity fixed right away or make an appointment in a week or so, or even put it off for months if you don't have dental insurance. The conditions underlying your experience could change greatly due to the delay—it could even result in complications that lead to even worse problems.

Naturally, it's more difficult to design something whose completion can vary. However, you can find ways to provide good customer experiences no matter how people move through an offering. For example, early online service applications typically required you to fill out an entire form before submitting it. Many people would get distracted halfway through or need to leave before completing it. Then they'd have to repeat the whole process again, from the beginning, when they could return to the task.

A lot of progress has been made since then. Some forms save your work on every page, allowing you to pick up where you left off if you have to stop before you're finished. Others autofill items based on preferences stored in your browser. A few even borrow login and profile information from social media sites to do the same. Similar principles can apply to everything from a retail store that supports its customers with product search kiosks to hospitals that send prescriptions automatically to the onsite pharmacy, making it easy to move quickly from your doctor's office out the door.

Likewise, this time variability can flow through multiple media and touchpoints. You can see this in brands that allow you to start a purchase on your home phone, continue it on your mobile phone, modify it on a website, and complete it when you pick the product up in a store. If the system governing and enabling the experience isn't designed to flow across time, media, and touchpoints gracefully, it will frustrate customers. If it works seamlessly, the opposite will occur. The key is that each touchpoint needs to continue the experience while behaving in ways that are appropriate to its particular platform.

What Design Needs from the Rest of the Organization

Although you've isolated an innovation team, design never happens in a vacuum—and shouldn't. But there are ways an organization can support creative innovation and ways it can greatly impede it. Even if management is not directly involved in the innovation process, it does need to recognize a few things:

- **Everyone will have an opinion.** Everyone is a design critic. It comes naturally because we all use products and services ourselves. The important point is to manage these opinions. Early on, those outside the design group may not be able to see with the vision of those inside. They may identify problems that seem intractable, but for which the team already has good solutions. For the most part, outside interference, especially early on, should be kept to a minimum.

- **Don't worry about early prototypes.** Designers have a big secret: the first version of something is invariably bad. You have to either look through to the finish line yourself, or failing that, trust that the process will yield something great.

- **Time matters.** Good design emerges over time as prototypes are built, tested, and iterated. One of the biggest mistakes organizations can make is to evaluate innovation efforts too early and hold them to unrealistic standards and expectations.

- **The process is ambiguous and cacophonous.** Design does not proceed in an easy, straightforward fashion. It cannot be plotted and ordered in the sense that accounting and manufacturing can. It sometimes moves in fits and starts, with long periods where you bang your heads against the wall or can't see the finished solution clearly before breakthroughs are made.

In other words, patience is the order of the day. If you give the design process time to wind its way through its usual torturous path, you'll usually be rewarded with good results.

EYE OPENERS

This chapter offered an overview of one of the most critical phases of relationship innovation: design. Although it did not go into exhaustive detail about the process, you saw that design consists of four major, interrelated activities: concept development, prototyping, testing, and iteration. You first devise potential solutions; then build rough-and-ready models of what the solution looks like; and finally test them. You then use that information to make improvements and continue the cycle of building and testing until you get a product or service that's customer-ready.

You also saw that designers should not design for themselves, but should primarily draw on the triggers uncovered in the discovering phase. They should take these insights as guidance and feel free to interpret and find creative solutions within them. Finally, you saw that the rest of the company needs to remain patient, especially early on, as prototypes will not necessarily work very well, and it will be hard to visualize the end result.

Some questions to help your company start talking:

- What kinds of expertise does your company need on its design team? Who needs to be involved and how often?

- Do you have a preferred process, or should you look into alternative ones to jump-start your innovation efforts?

- How well would your management respond to a rough prototype that didn't work very well?

- Is there a way you could create space for innovators to work through a messy process?

11

Delivering

Congratulations! At this point in the process, you've designed new solutions. Now it's time to deliver on the relationship. Obviously, much of getting a solution into customers' hands is a tactical exercise. It varies widely for different organizations, and is not really a central concern of this book (though you should do it well).

Instead, this chapter focuses more on the strategic side of *delivering*. A relationship requires making promises during the innovation process and then delivering on them. Your efforts mean nothing if the organization doesn't stay committed to producing the new experiences your customers want.

In essence, delivering involves executing on the experience statement you developed during the declaring phase and ensuring that everyone in the organization understands what it means and how it affects them. You also monitor actively to ensure that they act consistently to support that objective—and then you innovate to improve even more.

More than anything, though, delivering is about realizing the vision you've developed earlier in the innovation process by serving up the touchpoints you've designed to create experiences for customers. This phase, to a large extent, involves a handover of the process to the people most capable of executing on manufacturing, service delivery, ad production and placement, and so on. These individuals will need to develop a rollout plan that's highly tactical in nature. At the same time, the rest of the innovation team shouldn't just pick up their toys and go home. Careful, real-time review of execution as it unfolds is essential, for the three following reasons:

- Ensuring that the driving vision is being maintained.

- Using the execution process as a whole new set of opportunities to influence the evolution of the organization's culture.

- Observing customer response as a source of inspiration about the next set of innovations that will continue to drive the customer relationship forward, as well as improving the new touchpoints' ability to deliver on the experiences people want.

A Delivering Fail

One of the more spectacular failures at the delivering phase came with Microsoft's Zune player, which competed with the iPod. The product was ridiculed when released in 2006, sold poorly through several years, and was discontinued in 2011. However, something odd happened since it came to its ignominious end. People tried the product out of curiosity and came to the conclusion that it wasn't that bad. Appreciation rose.

It soon achieved cult status. And in 2012, it won a *Slate* reader poll of outdated technology worth a second look. Even today, sales of Zunes take place frequently on eBay, and sometimes with prices higher than they originally fetched.

It wasn't that Microsoft delivered a bad product. Aesthetically, it may not have matched its rivals, but it was intuitive and worked better in some ways. It had a music delivery model, for example, that was much more generous. (You got all the music you wanted for a low yearly subscription fee.) Granted, you lost it all when you stopped subscribing. It even had an FM radio, which some people liked.

The main problem, of course, was that Apple was delivering an ecosystem, not just a product, and they were already building relationships with iPod buyers. As we explained in the last chapter, you can't compete with an ecosystem if you're only delivering an MVP (minimally viable product). The Zune was a little bit more than an MVP but not by much. The iPod was already dominant, with tons of accessories and apps. Microsoft compounded the problem because it didn't deliver its product very well. It didn't build a relationship. Its advertising was spotty and haphazard. Its messaging was inconsistent and unclear. The Zune's advantages weren't clearly communicated, and no one got the sense of community they got from an iPod. Microsoft had delivered a product, but not a relationship.

Here's the moral of this story: making a great product or offering a great service is not enough. You have to understand that it sits in the context of a larger objective. If you don't provide the proper and consistent support across the entirety of your waveline diagram, your customers' experiences with it will be poor. This is because your offerings fit into their entire lives—and must fit well—not the other way around.

Getting Everyone on Board

When it comes to adapting your organization to deliver better relationships, a lot of the work has already been done. In the declaring phase, you created an experience statement that showed everyone abstractly what they needed to do. Now, it's time to revisit that document and use it as a framework for moving forward with the newly completed solution via a rollout plan. Just as you prepared everyone in the organization for the new relationship, now you have to ensure that they live up to that promise.

Putting together a rollout plan is, in some ways, the easiest part of the process, because most organizations are designed to execute on tactics, be they to finish manufacturing a new offering, work with an agency to complete a series of ads, or develop protocols for service delivery. What's different here isn't the nature of these plans, just the need to share them with the entire innovation team, to ensure that everyone's on the same page about where execution is headed.

When you're happy with your rollout plan, you need to implement the experience across the organization. This is a multistep process that includes:

- **Communicate the experience statement.** Whether you post it on a wall, make it a screen saver, or conduct workshops so that people understand it, you need to make sure everyone in the organization is aware of the experiences you intend to deliver.

- **Develop company-wide guidelines.** Your goal is to deliver experiences that build relationships with customers. To understand *how* you do this, develop guidelines for interaction. These are not laws or hard-and-fast rules, as you'll see. They are signposts that allow you to understand how you must act and react to customers in order to produce certain experiences.

- **Set departmental guidelines, too.** Naturally, every group in your organization will have different ways they can support the experiences you're trying to deliver. Sales can deliver *oneness* one way, service another. If you want to produce *wonder* at an amusement park, you want to immerse people in an amazing environment as soon as possible. (This does not mean that maintenance and housekeeping have to be full of wonder, too. Most likely, they should be obsessive and invisible.)

- **Incentivize the guidelines.** It's usually better to give people positive reasons to follow guidelines rather than negative consequences for not following them. Select employees who are doing particularly well and reward them publicly to demonstrate to all that you're serious about change.

- **Give your people flexibility.** When employees have their guidelines, give them leeway to make judgments to improve customer relationships. People aren't assembly lines or products, and their rules of engagement should not be solid or inflexible. When customer service people are limited in their ability to speak to and deal with customers (using set scripts with no deviation), their ability to improve the situation is limited.

- **Don't force the relationship on everyone.** Put simply, the customer is not always right. In implementing the relationship, don't allow your people to be abused simply to keep things going. Unacceptable behavior is exactly that and shouldn't be tolerated. When you do tolerate it, you're telling your employees that they don't matter and saying to your customers that anything goes. Neither builds the kinds of relationships you need to improve the experience over the long haul.

The final point is that you have to be consistent and maintain the relationship over time. Part of the challenge is that most organizations these days are split into silos or separate departments, largely for reasons of convenience or efficiency. The silos don't necessarily communicate with one another; they often are working at cross-purposes, and their incentives are all over the place. Unfortunately, they may all affect the experience or relationship.

Obviously, it would be difficult to reorganize an entire organization simply to reflect the experiences that customers want (though, ultimately, that's probably the best strategy an organization can have to develop long-term premium value). Instead, we recommend that your innovation team be composed of a wide range of stakeholders from every area that affects the customer relationship, at least in the beginning. They've worked together for months and know how all the moving parts of the company affect relationships. As a result, they can lead the effort to coordination between usually disparate entities.

Working Outside of Your Organization

In many cases, however, you will not control all touchpoints in your customer relationships. Rather, your partners will. And this can create additional challenges.

For example, a few years ago, Steve's company was hired by a vending machine company. It wanted to provide an extremely convenient experience for its customers. It had designed its machines with simple touchscreens, made them accessible via a wide range of payment types, and placed them in stores and other locations around the United States.

The problem was that people did not find them convenient. Knowing this, the company hired Steve's team to understand why. It turns out the failure had nothing to do with the company. It had done many good things to foster a relationship. The problem was that it allowed other people—those who owned the property—to determine where they were located. For whatever reason, those people were in the habit of placing the machines in the most inconvenient locations imaginable. They were often hard to find, sandwiched between racks, put behind boxes, or placed in areas frequently trafficked by employees. As a result, people found the machines anything but convenient. They were, instead, a hassle.

This example shows what can happen when someone else is in charge of selling your goods and services. They, too, contribute to the experiences your company evokes, and they, too, must be brought into alignment with your new promise.

Of course, doing so is not as straightforward a process as making your organization ready to deliver the new relationship. In Steve's client's case, his team was able to create instructional materials for those who hosted the machines, so they would understand how to display them properly. They also performed research that demonstrated the increased revenue a store might get from doing so. In your case, the carrots and sticks will likely be different, but it's important to deliver as consistent an experience as you can.

Monitoring Experience: Qualitative Measures

The final task in delivering involves making sure that you're keeping on track. Start by remembering how easy it is to kid yourself into thinking you're doing well. In Chapter 6, "Distancing and Team Structure," for example, you met a group of auto industry executives who felt they knew their customers' experience simply because they all drove their company's cars. Obviously, that wasn't the case.

Instead of trusting your gut feelings, there are a variety of ways of monitoring how well you're doing. Typically, they fall into two categories: quantitative and qualitative. Our view is that the latter is much better for monitoring experience. Make sure that you focus on the types of experiences the company is seeking to evoke in people—and that's a qualitative thing. It's hard to get at with numbers.

In doing qualitative research, revisit the techniques from the discovering phase (Chapter 7, "Discovering"). Especially useful are activities like metaphor and role-play, both of which are good at telling you how well you're doing at each point in the relationship. In addition, every company has its own opportunities to see how it's doing, such as the following examples. The following is by no means a full list.

- **Mystery shoppers.** Some retailers employ mystery shoppers to gain insights into employee performance. We advise doing this, but mainly for the purposes of understanding the customer relationship, not evaluating and possibly punishing employees. That said, if you are concerned that your employees are slacking off or stealing, you should obviously deal with it.

- **Call center employees.** The people manning customer service lines often have the most vital insights about customer touchpoints of anyone in a company. If you have a customer service department, checking with them, listening to their experiences, and possibly even sitting in on their calls should be a formal part of research and assessment.

- **Working the line.** Famously, the CEO of JetBlue works as a flight attendant one day each year. This is a great way to understand how things are going and keep track of the customer experience. Another way to do this is to rotate key employees through departments. For example, before MBA programs became popular, there were internal management training programs at most large companies. General Motors, for example, shuttled its best prospects through every division of the company's operations, including time on the assembly line and greeting customers in a dealership. By spending time on the front lines, managers can understand how the customer relationship is going.

Quantitative Measures

Obviously, qualitative measurement requires an investment in time and energy, and often money. And although there's a tendency to over-rely on quantitative measures, they can provide you with quicker insight and allow you to more closely monitor how you're doing on a short-term basis. Some of the better tools include:

- **Social satisfaction.** Social satisfaction is determined by what people are saying online about your company and whether it is positive or negative. Obviously, it's not the perfect way to measure how happy people are with a product or service, but changes in such metrics can be an indicator of progress.

- **Retention metrics.** With improved relationships, you should also see increases in the number of customers who come back for more.

- **Usage statistics.** The more you work on relationships, the more often people are likely to use your products and services. This is especially true for digital properties like apps, where you're trying to build a closer, more intimate conversation with your customers.

- **Customer service surveys (and why to avoid them).** Many companies now routinely send email to customers, requesting that they take a brief survey to measure their satisfaction and believing that this technique is better than doing nothing. From our vantage point, however, these surveys can be worse than doing nothing, primarily because a measurement of satisfaction doesn't provide any sort of guidance as to how to improve customer experience. The more precisely you can measure how customers' states of mind are affected by your offerings and touchpoints, the better you can course-correct.

- **Big data.** One exciting development in quantitative monitoring is to build a picture of customer experience by tying various databases of customer contact together. These might include customer service, customer relationship management (CRM), customer transactions, marketing contacts, sales records, digital analytics, third-party data, and surveys. This approach brings together multiple viewpoints to paint a better picture of customer behavior. It is in a state of rapid development and well worth watching as the tools reach maturity.

The Ultimate Measures

In the end, however, you will likely find the traditional measures best for knowing how you're doing. If you're doing well with relationships, your company should thrive. That's why you should also look at the following over time:

- **Stock price.** An increased market and press awareness about your innovation efforts can contribute to an increase in stock price. Obviously, you'll know for sure what is producing that rise, but if analysts are talking about you as an innovator, chances are you'll see an improvement.

- **Revenue and profit.** Revenue and profit are trickier concepts than you might think. For example, analysts have sometimes said that Apple would fall behind or lose its phone business unless it increased market share. This is an easy metric to measure and, as such, can become a stand-in for success. It can also be misleading. Whereas Apple quickly lost market share to Android-based phones, it maintained a lock on profits in the smartphone market. In fact, as we write this, Apple is still scooping up over 90 percent of the profits in the entire global market for smartphones, despite its relatively low market share. Ultimately, that's a better measure of the company's success.

- **Premium value.** The ultimate measurement for success, of course, is premium value. This emerges over a longer time period as people come to view your company differently. Thanks to your improved relationship with them, you can eventually charge more for what you provide than others doing the same. It takes a little courage to inch your prices above the average, but if your conversations with customers tell you they're ready, then you're finally reaching your real goal. Just don't expect this to happen overnight.

Starting Over

People change. Circumstances change. Hairstyles change. And relationships change. That's why full-scale relationship research should be periodically renewed and redone. That way you keep on top of your customers' wants and needs.

Do more research as often as you can. Relationship innovation needs to be a continual process that is pursued as much as is practical. As soon as you implement a new plan, it's time to roll up your sleeves, distance a team from your product and processes, and go back to work. Every release of a product or service is simply a prototype, as mentioned earlier. Only by continuing to innovate and improve can you hope to deepen and improve your relationships over time.

EYE OPENERS

Delivering is obviously a critical step in relationship innovation. You can make the best and most intriguing products in the world, but they will fail if you do not take the right steps to support them. These steps can be purely tactical, like manufacturing and marketing. But they also can include a number of softer steps that align your organization with the new vision. Some questions to get you thinking:

- How good is your company at delivering products or services?
- What sorts of guidelines for interaction have you come up with that make sense for your brand?
- What kinds of delivery-related research could you do that is unique to your company?
- What kinds of quantitative measures would work for you?
- What do you need to do to ensure that your team can be ready for constant innovation?

12

A World of Premium Value

This final chapter looks at relationship innovation from a different perspective: the effects it can have on businesses, people, and society as a whole. We believe firmly that improving relationships does not merely affect businesses. Whereas it creates premium value for companies over time, it also has a larger purpose. It improves lives. It makes things better.

The following pages present a world of premium value, one in which companies deliver valued relationships with their customers, and how those relationships can serve as catalysts for broader and better social change.

Moving Toward a Better Business Relationship

In the first chapter of this book, we cited a story about a Comcast representative who refused to allow a customer to discontinue his service. While the incident was doubtless annoying, we also noted that most of Comcast's competitors were doing the same thing.

Comcast and its competitors have for years made massive profits by delivering an essential service while making people unhappy. Consumers are forced to use their products; they cause us irritation and annoyance. As a result, they invite negative relationships with users, and customers are ready to switch to a competing service or solution at a moment's notice. In addition, Comcast and its competitors (where they have them) constantly battle each other on price and performance, undercutting each other to gain or keep a customer. They aren't able to generate significant premiums because the value on which that premium would be based doesn't exist.

This issue is indicative of a broader problem, not just in business, but in society as well. When the focus is only on financial and functional value, anyone can lose not only the ability to capture premium value, but also the ability to satisfy people in deep, meaningful ways. When social commentators talk about contemporary life becoming more "transactional," they mean that it seems to increasingly focus only on basic value, at the expense of emotional satisfaction and fulfillment of identities and relationships to the world.

This doesn't have to be the case, of course, and it wasn't always so. The U.S. economy has accomplished something unprecedented in human history—through unprecedented efficiencies and productivity—it has the capacity to meet the functional needs of virtually everyone, worldwide. If it doesn't yet do so, it's not for lack of production capacity; it's because of differences in resources available to each person to acquire them.

Ironically, the very functionalist mindset that made this economic miracle possible simultaneously contributed to an impoverishment for most when it comes to premium value in life. The functionalist focus has done this in many ways, directly through the substitution of basic value for premium value. It also does this indirectly by convincing us to enact policies, processes, and metrics that further reinforce the dominance of basic value.

For example, look at the chart in the figure. It features two lines. The one at the top measures the U.S. gross domestic product (GDP) from 1929 to 2010. As you can see, it has steadily risen over the last six decades, and, as a result, the country, as a whole, has gotten wealthier. The second line is a different measure: the genuine progress indicator (GPI). This is a different measure that also takes into account social and environmental factors. For example, if the poverty rate increases, it impacts the GPI. So does divorce, pollution, illness, and a host of other factors. Think of GDP as financial and functional value (only) and GPI as an attempt to quantify premium value (though it has a long way to go before it truly measures emotional, identity, and meaningful value). It's not a complete measure of premium value, but it's the closest we have so far.

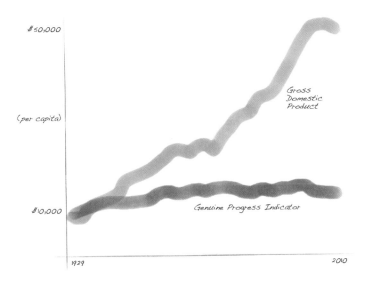

Still, this diagram shows that as the financial value of the United States has skyrocketed, the premium value in our lives has declined. A few companies and individuals are making more and more money and the country (as a whole) is increasing its economic output, but at an increasing cost in quality of life. A family of four used to be able to live comfortably on one parent's earnings, whereas now two-income earners only scrape by. The emotional reality many feel lies in stark contrast to the rosy economic picture painted by quantitative metrics. By paying attention only to the bottom line without asking about those types of value that are harder to measure, you miss the impact on premium value throughout your markets and lives. Ultimately, this impacts even the economy as people pull back, scrimp, and try to save rather than invest. This goes against popular business thinking (for the last 70 years), but the statistics prove it out.

Another way to measure quality of life is to simply poll people about their happiness. Admittedly, this only gets at a part of emotional value (but an important part). But it gives you another indicator of premium value. In fact, surveys typically report that societies with the highest GDPs rank near the bottom in happiness—so much so that there is already a new metric in development: gross national happiness (GNH). In other words, by focusing solely on creating functional and economic value, premium value appears to be destroyed, or at least underinvested in. And premium value is what's most important. After there's enough money for people to eat and feel reasonably secure, the emotional, identity, and meaningful parts of their daily lives mean much more than the financial and functional. As mentioned earlier in the book, when people go through exercises to describe the most important object they own, they almost never choose the most expensive. Emotional, identity, and meaningful value almost always trump basic value. Yet, most businesses seek only to measure and pay attention to the things that matter least to their customers. Charted together, you can see a story of what happens in your life when premium value loses out to basic.

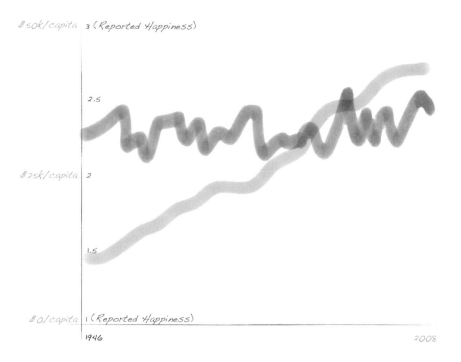

$50k/capita 3 (Reported Happiness)

2.5

$25k/capita 2

1.5

$0/capita 1 (Reported Happiness)

1946   2008

What really matters in peoples' lives may feel more ethereal, but it's still quite real, and those organizations that focus their efforts there stand to fill a lucrative void that immensely satisfies their clients (and that they're willing to pay for). In short, this is an opportunity for companies to provide premium value.

New Management Tools

To be successful at delivering premium value, businesses need better management tools, not merely better measurement, design, and development tools. You can use wavelines to develop better relationships that provide more premium value, but these aren't helpful in measuring and managing that value day to day throughout the rest of business. If every decision businesses make is governed only by financial and functional considerations, then only those lesser kinds of value can result.

That much is clear. In addition, truly successful innovation requires an understanding of customers and partners on other, deeper levels. The best companies are those that manage to make successful relationship decisions, in spite of the fact that they lack hard numbers to guide their decisions. The companies that have survived the longest, those that have the best reputations and the most loyal customers, aren't those merely reducing every policy, offering, and decision down to what they can easily measure. They have also learned that, in spite of the ephemeral nature of premium value, it significantly impacts the most important measure of all—dollars and cents paid by customers.

What to do, then? We've maintained throughout this book that, even in the absence of premium value measurement techniques, companies can still overcome their blind spots and deliver this value by detecting the demand for it through new approaches to consumer research, identify specific opportunities by generating wavelines, and build them into offerings through design principles imbued with them. That said, it would certainly be great if measurement tools could be invented.

Fortunately, some emerging tools for the actual measurement of premium value are appearing on the horizon. One possible tool is the elusive Integrated Bottom Line (IBL) accounting promoted by sustainability experts like Hunter Lovins. For over a decade, the sustainability community has been talking about IBL and managing the Triple Bottom Line,[1] but no one has created the tools to do so—yet. Part of this is because no one knows how to measure all of the facets of natural and human capital needed to fulfill this vision.

---

1. Triple Bottom Line refers to measuring the costs and benefits of natural capital (ecological impacts) and human capital (social impacts) in addition to financial capital. The challenge for those few companies that have tried it is by keeping these separate, in three different columns, it's too easy to ignore the two new columns when management gets difficult and the inherent relationships among three forms of capital are lost. Integrated Bottom Line is an improved approach that seeks to remove the separation so that the cause and effect of costs and benefits are always apparent.

So new research and measurement tools are needed as well. In addition, SASB, the sustainability-focused organization analogous to FASB (the Financial Accounting Standards Board that governs regulations around financial reporting), is making headway in developing new standards with similar outcomes.

Total Sales (Revenue)
Total Sales Costs
Gross Margin

Expenses:
Human Capital (inc. training costs/savings, employee retention, etc.)
Marketing (inc. Community & customer engagement costs & benefits, etc.)
Manufacturing (inc. resource costs, savings, & benefits, etc.)
Distribution (inc. transportation costs, savings, & benefits, etc.)
Rent (inc. costs & benefits)
Utilities (inc. energy costs, impacts, & savings, etc.)
Insurance (inc. mitigation costs, impacts & savings, etc.)
Total Operating Expenses

Gross Benefit
Taxes and Interest
Net Impact

For now, you need to suspend some disbelief, point to the cases where organizations have been successful, and invest in premium value ahead of having sophisticated, new tools to measure and manage it. In truth, this used to be how companies were run: metrics were just one of the ways an organization saw itself and its goals. Until it became the primary way, and now, often, the *only* way, leaders regularly cared about reputation, customer happiness, loyalty, and quality. It was only after sophisticated metrics became overwhelmingly popular with business analysts and stock pickers that leaders became convinced metrics of financial and functional value told the whole story, rather than just part of it. Looking to the future, it's vital to find ways to balance the value equation.

That said, these new premium value measurement tools need to be developed—another opportunity for an enterprising company.

Long-Term Focus on Relationships

It may sound a bit like we're arguing against financial and functional value, but we're not. What we're asking you to focus on is the relationships you create with your customers, employees, and partners (not to mention your friends and families). This is because relationships encompass total value: both basic and premium. When you truly keep relationships in the forefront of your mind, strategies, and tactics, you can't help but build value in both, and both strengthen and stabilize the relationships you hope to grow. To reach premium status, organizations must have a strategy that addresses all five forms of value, as well as implements on each throughout their operations.

In this way, everyone (and every business) is in the relationship business. It's not a special category for a few, select brands and organizations. If you don't believe this, it doesn't mean you're not doing it; it just means that you're likely creating marginal or even terrible relationships—because you're not tending to the ones you already have.

We recognize that it's difficult to manage factors you can't easily measure, but this doesn't change the fact that relationships already exist for all organizations, and that they need to be crafted and managed nonetheless.

In your personal life, acquaintances who don't provide real meaning and value rarely stay close for long. You lose touch with them because your relationship isn't positive. Nonetheless, we maintain unproductive relationships with businesses, because in spite of their intense branding efforts, they're seen as non-people who aren't supposed to participate in daily life. Most consumers think that organizations shouldn't touch them in a meaningful way, although they love those businesses that do.

We know that the value that companies gain from relationships often far outweighs the cost of gaining them. Relationships also stabilize a company's success over time; and companies can also monetize those relationships. As a result, a more enlightened, positive approach to customers not only is the right thing to do for them, but also the right thing to do for the business. Those companies that manage to build good relationships eventually reap financial rewards, as well. They can charge more, make more money, and even see their stock prices soar.

Traditional societies had no dearth of meaningful experiences and value. They got it from work, religion, family, art, nature, and so on. It may be that they inadvertently traded the premium value acquired from traditional sources for functional value in the attempt to rationalize their productive systems, putting efficient production ahead of the more intangible premium values. That doesn't mean that the productivity revolution is somehow tainted or inherently opposed to premium value, simply that it hasn't been the primary focus of modern institutions until recently. Ironically, the very corporations that spearheaded the productivity revolutions that have weakened society's focus on premium values are now being called upon to deliver that premium value. Corporations as well as governments and non-profits have been hesitant to claim impact here, but there's no reason not to do so.

Stock values show that many companies are already playing this game anyway, but they just do so mostly intuitively or even accidentally. And, sometimes, they have to fend off activist investors as they do.

The Bigger Picture

You may think that relationship innovation matters merely to a few businesses. But with top businesses reaping such great rewards for this, competitors are sure to follow. The last few years, for example, have seen a great increase in companies purchasing design firms and hiring designers. Facebook, Google, IBM, and others have all added significant design capabilities. Their goal is to make beautiful products and responsive services that are better aligned with what people want.

If this trend continues, it should begin to shape expectations around relationships. After all, if Facebook and Google join Apple, Disney, and others as strong relationship companies, they will create a situation where nearly every person in middle income and wealthy countries will have at least one strong relationship with a company. At that point, expectations will be set such that other companies will no longer be able to ignore relationships. They'll all have to create better relationships with their customers.

In turn, that may drive an increased need for relationship innovation in other places as well. The relationship approach should be applied to governments, agencies, and non-profits. Often, these entities don't approach relationships with their constituents as being of mutual, premium value. But the rewards that companies can gain doing so are analogous to those that all organizations can reap. Governments can serve their constituents in premium ways, not merely basic ones. In fact, doing so is likely to make them more stable and engender more trust, participation, and respect than those who don't. No organization can ignore functional and financial value (though many do), but ignoring premium value is a disservice to their potential customers.

All relationships are ever-evolving, making them more challenging to manage. Stop thinking of them as static interactions updated infrequently. That way of thinking was acceptable for a world with far less change and far fewer connections, but you don't live in such a world any longer. Recognizing this fact forces organizations of all types to confront the value they provide and innovate to deliver more of it.

On a Personal Level

What's unclear, however, is what effect this potential revolution in business relationships could have on personal ones. Would improved relationships between businesses and their customers set the stage for different relationships between people? Could organizations be used as a catalyst to remind us of the value we provide to each other in our personal lives?

You probably know people who look at relationships with others as most companies do with their customers, in starkly financial or functional terms. The stereotypes are plenty: the social climber who only wants to be seen with influential people in order to play off some of that influence; the spoiled child who only caters to his parents' needs in the hopes of gaining an inheritance; the trophy wife who has traded her desire for love to marry into a family with a pedigree; the friend who silently calculates favors, tit for tat, to maintain equilibrium. These are common but don't foster lasting, stable, fulfilling relationships. Few among us would prescribe such behavior to have a successful or satisfying life.

Yet, these are exactly the same approaches most companies take with their customers (and expect, in kind). In effect, businesses have been terrible friends to their customers (and, often, employees and partners) because their focus on only the material side of experience makes them just the kind of "people" no one wants to be around. Organizations vie for their customers' attention, time, and money but do little to earn them when they focus only on functional and economic value. It's really as simple as this: if you want good relationships, you need to be a good partner. If you want the best and most value out of those relationships, you need to invest in them in premium ways.

No matter how strong your relationships with businesses become, they will never be powerful enough to rival the relationships you build with your close family and friends—they simply can't consistently deliver the same quality of premium value, year in, year out, that those more traditional sources can. But commercial relationships raise the bar of your expectations and highlight the premium value you receive in your personal life and how special it is.

Ultimately, all of us, regardless of professions, are experience designers who seek to influence the experiences of others around us. We learn the basics of personal relationships as infants, when we first find we can influence other people's behavior with our own. Within a few years, virtually all of us develop a working knowledge of the fact that everyone around us has experiences, just like we do, and that we can influence these experiences for the better. Building personal relationships is, at its heart, no different from building professional or commercial ones, so long as we care not just for the outcome, but also for the people involved on each side of the relationship.

What commercial relationships can teach, however, is about the conscious mechanics of relationship building. Better knowledge of these mechanics, as well as their effects, can only illuminate how they work in our personal lives, allowing us to improve relationships across the board. Relationships don't just happen. They take work and are most successful when deliberate. Because organizations aren't people, and relationships don't come as naturally or easily. So, in their need to understand the process and act on it deliberately, you can uncover the mechanics of relationships that determine dynamic, mutual, premium value. In this way, organizational relationships might be able to create insights that lead you to better personal relationships—especially for those to whom relationships don't come naturally or easily.

Premium Value, Premium Society

On a societal level, this could also lead to new relationships in the public realm. By understanding citizens and constituents in premium ways, you might gain the ability to produce more satisfying interactions and policies and identify aspects of culture to promote, engage, and expand. Imagine a government agency that considers premium value alongside basic value when making decisions about its constituents. Perhaps, the value of a local landmark could more easily outweigh the revenue of yet another shopping mall? Perhaps, if organizations saw both the value to citizens and companies alike, in both premium and functional ways, better decisions would be made that benefit both.

We have yet to see, let alone understand, what a world focused on premium value might create. It surely wouldn't be a utopia, but it might be the closest we could come. When we have relationships that are close, supportive, and fulfill us on more valued levels (they make us feel good, they validate who we are, and they confirm our worldviews), we tend to be far less anxious, fearful, reactionary, or unstable. We're not as easily excited or swayed, and we're more thoughtful about the long term.

Perhaps we could then look to cultures around the world that score highly in terms of happiness and satisfaction and learn from them. We don't feel that this is a decision between tech and primitive cultures, or the developed and developing worlds. Premium value isn't the same as basic value, but neither are they mutually exclusive. In fact, premium value shows signs of amplifying and enhancing basic value so that even if we don't have as many things or as much basic value, we're still more satisfied and engaged.

So, if our lives are more filled with satisfaction and meaning, how does that affect the world? Does it make us more sustainable or less? Less materialistic or more? If companies provide more meaningful experiences and relationships in our lives, does this challenge traditional institutions (like churches and governments) or does it reinforce them? Does this make for happier citizens or does it have little to no impact?

All of this is speculation, at the moment, and we can't tell for sure. But, we're excited to find out. All we have to do is start trying. One thing for certain is that the more we see, the more we eliminate important blind spots and the better our decisions will be.

EYE OPENERS

Some final questions to ask yourself as you ponder engaging in a relationship-focused innovation process include:

- Ultimately, who do you want to be in your relationships with your customers?
- What will it take to inculcate this vision within your organization?
- How does your sense of your role at your company change if you fully embrace this approach?

Index

Acknowledgments

The authors wish to recognize a number of people who consented to be interviewed by or worked with us in the course of researching this book, most of whom probably never expected us to ever get this done! They include Barbara Denton, Patricia Jen, Robert Mangel, and their colleagues at Kaiser Permanente, who first introduced us to the strategic possibilities of designing evolving experiences, as well as Michael Caplan, Greg Delaune, Chris Deyo, Etienne Feng, Chap Freeman, Matt Greeley, Hudson, Pete Krammer, Adrien Lanusse, Catherine Lovazzano, Bryan Mahlmeister, Daniel Makoski, Ashley McCorkle, Jerry Michalski, Ryan Opina, Eric Ryan, George Simmons, Jacob Simmons, Pat Tickle, Michael Weaver, Shawn White, David Williams, and Susan Worthman.

We also acknowledge Steve's colleagues at Scansion, without whom many of the ideas in this book would never have reached fruition— Salvador Acevedo, Shawn Ardaiz, Alvin Cheung, John Garvie, JJ Hadley, Daniel Gomez Seidel, Tony Senna, Clynton Taylor, Robyn Waldruff, and Christine Young.

The inspiration for these ideas came to us from many sources. Along with those mentioned in the above paragraphs, we'd like to thank the students in the design MBA programs at California College of the Arts, who have used these tools and helped validate them with valuable feedback for the last six years. They are too numerous to name (over 300), but their experience with the waveline has given us valuable insight on how to describe and work with it.

The same is true for the students and collaborators at the University of Cincinnati School of Design, Art, Architecture, and Planning. Working with students in the undergraduate and graduate programs provided a practice field that over time aided in our discoveries. Thanks, also, to Sean's colleagues within design at Procter & Gamble where challenging the status quo was "accepted and added" with enthusiasm.

Innovation, radical ideas, thinking differently—whatever you like to call it—is rarely done alone. We have noted this above. But it is also rarely done without the support of those who are closest to you—those who won't leave you when it gets difficult. For that kind of support, Sean thanks his wife Wendy and daughter Jenna for their unwavering support and Steve thanks his partner, Ira Johnson.

We cannot thank Douglas Rushkoff enough for writing such a poignant foreword that helps set the context for why we wrote this book. We've admired his writing for a decade, and we're honored to have him contribute to our book.

Lastly, much thanks is due to our editors, Joe Shepter, Sue Hobbs, and Marta Justak, who helped make clear the thoughts in our heads and our publisher, Lou Rosenfeld for investing in this book. We're indebted to their work, time, and endless energy.

About the Authors

 STEVE DILLER leads Scansion, an innovation strategy firm that identifies, shapes, and builds experiences that transform markets and businesses. As an "experience strategist," Steve brings a unique perspective, rooted in the "time-based arts," such as film and music, as well as anthropology and cognitive psychology, that makes it possible to optimize any offering in an era of rapid technological and social change. His clients have ranged from the Fortune 100 to start-ups, including Autodesk, P&G, Chrysler, Logitech, Intel, Gannett, The Washington Post Co., The Economist Group, Carhartt, DirecTV, GM, Electrolux, Microsoft, and AAA.

Prior to forming Scansion, Steve was senior vice-president of brand strategy at Added Value, and before that was a partner and director of innovation at Cheskin. Before Cheskin, he owned a film production company and produced and directed several feature films. Steve is also a founding member of the faculty at California College of the Arts' MBA in Design Strategy program, teaching Market Insights and Social Ventures.

Steve received a Master's Degree in Public Policy Studies from the University of Chicago, a Bachelor's Degree in History from Carleton College, and a Bachelor's Degree in Film from Columbia College. With Nathan and Darrel Rhea, he co-authored *Making Meaning: How Successful Businesses Deliver Meaningful Customer Experiences*, and has contributed to *Trust: Das Prinzip Vertraue* and *The Human-Computer Interaction Handbook*.

You can reach Steve at steve@scansion.com.